RESEARCH METHODS:

A Synthesized Framework

Emeka Nwabueze

DEDICATION

To my daughter

Priscilla Mmutaka Njoku

PREFACE

This book derives largely from many years of teaching Research Methods at both undergraduate and postgraduate levels and in different academic disciplines. The experience convinced me of the need for a synthesized approach to the study of this interesting subject. The resort to manuals of various types contributed, to a large extent, in making the study of research methodology enigmatic to students. Sometimes, some of these manuals are principally designed to see the student through the requirements of the prescribed degree, while others make the erroneous assumption that teaching the methods of documentation as prescribed by a particular school constitutes the complete requirement for the study of research methods.

The problem generally stems from the way research is introduced to students. Within a short period of time, they are expected to decide on a research method to be used: historical, analytical, descriptive, empirical, experimental, Bibliometric, or other esoteric vocabularies equally frightening. The course they took in Research Methodology hardly addressed such concepts, and the entire course undoubtedly did not have the blessing of abundant scholarship because it was probably not taught by a practicing researcher. Interdisciplinarity, a characteristic feature of contemporary scholarship, may not even have been stressed. Hence, there is absolutely no doubt that a book of this nature has been missing on the shelves of our university libraries.

The idea for the text originated with the students who have persistently challenged me with the fact that they needed a text that would provide comprehensive guidance on the subject of research. It is with this perceived need that this practical book, a quintessence of methodical minimalism, was conceived. This book, therefore, encompasses a wide range of illuminating ideas and methods designed to help not only the student researcher but also other scholars of diverse academic disciplines. It is designed to make its readers recognize that research is not merely a body of knowledge to be learned but a set of activities to be performed.

Despite the fact that this synthesized approach to research methodology derives principally from my experience in teaching research methods in many institutions around the globe, it also benefited from discussions about research with faculty and students in these institutions.

I am indebted to the superb advice and warm encouragement of some of my colleagues: Professor Patrick O. Ngoddy from the University of Nigeria, Professor Sam C. Ukala of Delta State University, Professor Briant Hamor Lee, my mentor at Bowling Green State University, Ohio U.S.A Professor Oscar G. Brockett of the University of Texas at Austin, Professor Nick E. Muoneke of Prairie View A & M University, Professor Peter Nazareth of the University of Iowa, and Professor Ken Julien, President, University of Trinidad and Tobago, I am also grateful to my undergraduate and postgraduate students at the University of Nigeria, Nsukka, Edward Waters College, Jacksonville, Florida, Randolph College, Lynchburg, Virginia, The University of Swaziland, Kwaluseni, Imo State University, and the University of Trinidad and Tobago, who have been harassing me for a book of this magnitude.

Finally, I thank my wife, Chii, and all my children who have always given me delightful cooperation whenever I am engaged in serious academic work, especially when I have a deadline to keep. My wife, a professional Accountant, has, out of love for my intellectual harvest, developed a tremendous interest in the Humanities. My children, who are my greatest aficionados and critics, know when I need to be incommunicado and willingly suspend asking for their paternal rights until the coast becomes clear.

CONTENTS

Dedication

Preface

Chapter One

INTRODUCTION TO THE RESEARCH PROCESS

Argumentum

The Meaning of Research

Categories of Research

Normative Research and the Scientific Method

The Purpose of Research

Qualities of a Good Researcher

Chapter *Two*

SELECTING A RESEARCH TOPIC

The Researcher's Interest

Availability of Research Materials

Researcher's Knowledge of the Topic

Subjective/Controversial Topics

Manageability of the Topic

Time Factor

Topics to be Avoided

Narrowing Down the Topic

Developing a Thesis

Chapter Three

GATHERING INFORMATION

The Development of Writing

The Development of the Library

The Use of the Library in Research

Library Classification Systems

Finding Information

The Domino Theory

Assembling a Working Bibliography

Checking the Usefulness of a Book

Evaluating Research Sources

Selecting sources

Internet Sources

Advantages and Disadvantages of the Internet

Search Engines

Chapter Four

THE RESEARCH OUTLINE

Meaning

Elements of the Outline

Types of Outlines

Composing the Outline

Choice of Outline

General Model of an Outline

Decimal Notation of the Outline

Generic Method

Revision Checklist

Chapter Five

THE RESEARCH PROPOSAL

Classification of Scholarly Activities

Characteristics of Critical Thinking

Investigation (Fact Finding)

Critical Interpretation

Final Conclusion or Judgement

Preliminary Statements

The Hypothesis

Significance of the Problem

Definitions, Assumptions and Limitations

A Brief Review of Related Literature

Theoretical Framework

The Research Procedure

Time Schedule

Chapter Six

REVIEW OF SCHOLARSHIP

Chronological Arrangement

Thematic Arrangement

Methodological Arrangement

Categorical Arrangement

Sources to be Reviewed

Writing a Good Review of Scholarship

Chapter Seven

INVESTIGATIVE TECHNIQUES

Documentary Research

Reasons for Undertaking Documentary Research

Sources of Materials for Documentary Research

Critical Evaluation of Sources

Biographical Criticism Versus Deconstruction

Biographical Criticism

Deconstruction

HISTORICAL RESEARCH

Basic Characteristics of Historical Research

Collection of Data in Historical Research

EXPERIMENTAL RESEARCH

Categories of Experimental Research

SURVEY RESEARCH METHOD

Cross-sectional and Longitudinal Surveys

Sampling Procedures

Random Sampling

Stratified Sampling

Double Sampling

Cluster Sampling

Steps in Designing a Sample

THE INTERVIEW

Steps in Conducting an Interview

Recording

THE QUESTIONNAIRE

Definition

Designing a Good Questionnaire

Validation of the Questionnaire

OBSERVATIONAL RESEARCH

Definition

Necessity for Observational Research

Ethical Considerations in Observational Research

Observational Variables

Types of Observations

Major Differences

Critical and Pre-critical Response to Observation

PARTICIPANT OBSERVATION

Meaning

History and Development of Participant Observation

Difference between Observation and Participant Observation

Difficulties in Participant Observation

Advantages of Participant Observation

CONTENT ANALYSIS

Definition

Coding

Conceptual Analysis

Relational Analysis

Uses of Content Analysis

Advantages of Content Analysis in the Research Process

Main Disadvantages

BIBLIOMETRICS RESEARCH

Definition

Areas of Bibliometrics Research

Laws of Bibliometrics Research

EXPLORATORY RESEARCH

Meaning

Sources of Exploratory Research

Purpose of Exploratory Research

DIALECTICAL RESEARCH

Meaning

Method

Chapter Eight

WRITING THE RESEARCH REPORT

Sections of the Report

The Reference Section

Writing the First Draft

Development of Paragraphs

The Rhetorical Method

Writing Time

Style

Organization

Presenting Arguments

Writing Good Arguments

Rhetorical Appeals that Shape Arguments

Things to Avoid in Stating an Argument

Scientific Writing (The Laboratory Report)

Revision Techniques

Steps to Effective Revision

Re-examination of the Content

Re-evaluation of Ideas

Check on Language

Tone

Consistency

Transitional Connections

Checking for Noise

Ensuring Appropriate Use of Verbs

Accuracy of Paraphrases

Final Checking

Chapter Nine

DOCUMENTATION

Definition

Systems of Documentation

MODERN LANGUAGES ASSOCIATION (MLA)

Comment or Content Notes

Parenthetical Citations

Major Differences

In-text Citation

Introducing an Authority

Citing More Than One Work by the Same Author

More than One Work by the Same Author

Work by Two or Three Authors

Work by More Than Three Authors

Work by an Unknown Author

Work by a Corporate Author

Multivolume Work

Poetry, Drama and the Bible

Constitution

Quote of a Quote

General Guidelines

Documenting Journal Articles

Reference Works

OnLine Books, Articles, And Documents

AMERICAN PSYCHOLOGICAL ASSOCIATION (APA)

In-text Citation

Reference list

Journal Articles

Internet Sources

The Number Systems

The Medical Sciences

Computer

Mathematics

Physics and Engineering,

Citation Sequence for In-text Citations

Citation Sequence for In-text Citation Using Name-Year Method

Preparing a Reference List

Preparing a Reference List

CHICAGO MANUAL OF STYLE (CMS)

In-text Citations

Footnotes and Endnotes

Creating the Superscript

Preparing Footnotes on CMS Format

Preparing Endnotes

Preparing a Bibliography

Summary: General Hints on Documentation

Punctuation

Placement on In-text Citation

Length Quotations

Missing Information

CHAPTER TEN –

PLAGIARISM

Meaning of Plagiarism

Intentional Unintentional Plagiarism

Reason for Plagiarism

Penalty for Plagiarism

Methods of Avoiding Plagiarism

Chapter Eleven

Writing the Abstract

Meaning

Length of Abstracts

Valuable Hints on Writing the Abstract

Qualities of a Good Abstract

Chapter Twelve

A GLOSSARY OF RESEARCH TERMS

References

Index

One

INTRODUCTION TO THE RESEARCH PROCESS

Research is formalized curiosity.

It is poking and prying with a purpose.

- Zora Naele Hurston

It seems probable that a good deal of the trauma people experience in the presence of research may be attributable to the way research is traditionally approached and especially the way it is introduced to our students.

- David Addington

Empirical Research in Theatre

Argumentum

Research is an indispensable part of scholarship, and its investigative techniques are as old as the development of knowledge. By the sixth century BC, when Greek philosophy began, the Olympian religion was already on the decline, though it continued to ignite great inspiration in art and architecture. Significant scholars like Aristotle and Plato flourished. The Great Dialogues of Plato and the scholarly writings of Aristotle posed significant questions on what constituted ultimate truth. The answer to these questions led to the invention of methods of thinking and through these unique methods, definite answers emerged. Through the intellectual works of Aristotle and Plato, as well as those of the Pre-Socratic philosophers of the earlier century, the mental process of reaching reality, the process of reasoning, began to flourish.

Greek philosophy and critical thinking pre-dated science. Science, meaning knowledge, was indeed a part of the philosophical process. It involved information gathering, preferably from observation and using reason to analyze and interpret them.

One of the questions that occupied the minds of pre-Socratic philosophers was how to arrive at the ultimate reality. It was the analysis of this important philosophical question that led Thales of Miletus to declare, in 500 BC, that water was the original substance that preceded everything else. Another philosopher countered this by claiming that fire was the original substance. A third philosopher further challenged the two great thinkers by maintaining that the four elements - earth, water, fire, and air - were all created by a prior substance, which he described as the "boundless unknown".

It is clear that these thinkers were significantly engaged in a scientific quest, with pure conviction that it was possible to interpret the universe. The most significant answer during this period was given by two sixth-century philosophers, Democritus and Leucippus when they applied the term "atom" to what was earlier described as the ultimate substance. Atom, they insisted, meant something which cannot be divided.

Socrates and Plato rejected the claim that certainty dwelt in the observation and explanation of natural things. Plato, known for his copious analytical thought, rejected the study of nature, the Greek word for Physics. Rather, he engaged in a search for reality, which he felt existed beyond nature and which, he thought, could be interpreted through a higher intellectual ability, which he described as reason. Reason, he insisted, leads to truth which he considered perfect knowledge because it dealt with ideas.

Aristotle, born in Macedonia in present-day Northern Greece, was profoundly interested in science and was the inventor of the concept of causality – an explanation of why things happen. Aristotle went into metaphysics later, advocating the need for a balance between empiricism and formation. He contributed immensely to human thought and categorized human thought into analytical areas like politics, ethics, aesthetics, science and metaphysics. Thus, the concept of knowledge continued to grow.

Despite all these innovations in the development of knowledge, many yawning gaps still existed and begged for explanation. A major aspect of this was the search for evidence and proof of existence in all spheres of human life, including God. It was this state of scholarly analysis that led to the vehement declaration that unavailability of evidence does not necessarily mean evidence of total unavailability. The need to continue the search becomes inevitable, and that is what research is about. To understand it better, it is necessary to examine two aspects of learning.

Active and Passive Learning

Intellectual development involves two methods of acquiring ultimate knowledge: passive and active learning. Passive learning involves exposure of facts through lectures, seminars, and discussions. Here, the recipient is given information without active participation in the source of the information. In this method, information is given from the teacher to the learner, often without any resort in discussions or other transactional activities. This kind of learning often leads to spoon-feeding and rote learning. Examples of passive learning abound in lectures, listening to podcasts or watching videos.

Active learning, on the other hand, involves engaging learners in participatory activities, interactive learning, and self-directed situations aimed at helping the learner think critically about what is being learned with the aim of developing the ability to synthesize issues, engage in a deeper understanding of the issues being studied, and develop their own ideas.

As a systematic inquiry into particular areas of knowledge, it involves the location and utilization of information, analysis and interpretation of material so located, and the examinations of issues with the aim of making pertinent conclusions. Active learning, therefore, gives rise to research.

The Meaning of Research

The word research is derived from the French word *recherché,* which means to search closely and wisely. *Chercher* means "to search', and *re* suggests a repetition or continuous activity. The literal meaning of research, from its French etymology, means to study or investigate closely and thoroughly.

Glenn Legget, David Mead and William Charvat have argued that since the process of research "range all the way from simple fact-digging to the most obtuse speculations", there is no general definition of research that would apply faithfully to the research process.

Applying directly the meaning of research from its French etymology lays bare the most important parts of research. It has become fashionable to emphasize the two syllables in the word, research. The first syllable of the word, re, means to search critically and exhaustively, while the second syllable, search, means a systematic and methodological study whose ultimate aim involves the search for new knowledge or new interpretations of an existing one.

Research uses systematic methods to delve into the unknown in order to discover new facts. This implies that research needs to be orderly and systematic and requires a kind of methodology in its application. Evaluation of ideas and discovery of new knowledge, though very important in the research process, are not the only destinations of research.

The approach to research has to be critical and exhaustive, and the aim of the investigation is to discover new facts and convey the report faithfully and correctly in an acceptable method. It also involves the revision of accepted conclusions, whether they are in the form of theories or laws. Such revision should be in the light of the newly discovered facts or a copious re-examination of the conclusions, theories or laws. It is a copious investigation into a particular subject or topic, carried out systematically, with the aim of gaining a deeper understanding of existing knowledge or to derive new knowledge. Most researches involve both qualitative and quantitative approaches to the solution of a determined problem.

For research to take place, four important facts must be observed: it should be orderly and systematic, it should be complete, it involves the solution to a problem, and it aims at the discovery of new knowledge.

Research requires the application of a methodology that would lead the researcher to the solution of the research problem. This should be done in an orderly and systematic way. A carefully executed research leaves no questions unanswered within the major field of investigation. With this point in mind, the researcher should first identify a problem to be investigated, after which he delves into the distillation of the identified problem. Identification is the process of determining the research idea to be studied. Identification may result from one of the following:

1. a lacuna in the completed research available in the area of investigation;
2. no previous research available in the area of investigation;
3. previous research completed in the area has been poorly executed.

After problem identification, the researcher then faces the problem of distillation. This is the process of refining the problem and sifting the idea to make it investigatable. While doing this, care should be taken to ensure that the significance of the problem is clearly stated. This means that it should add new information to the existing state of knowledge and have advantages to others apart from the researcher.

Research, therefore, has a bipartite definition: a careful investigation into the unknown mainly for the purpose of discovery and an orderly and systematic way of searching again and again into the known for purposes of advancement, refinement and improvement.

Categories of Research

There are two major categories of research – **basic or fundamental**, or **pure** research and **applied** or **directed** research. Basic research also called fundamental or pure research, is an exploration into the unknown, sometimes undertaken without any practical conclusion in the mind of the researcher. The results of basic research are sometimes unexpected. Curiosity, interest, and intuition are the driving forces in basic research. It is undertaken by an investigator who has enough curiosity, intuition and interest to inquire into a particular phenomenon. This kind of investigation searches for new knowledge, the undiscovered, and usually supplies the applied researcher with pertinent information to advance his efforts. The basic researcher tries to establish the existence of a phenomenon.

Applied or directed research yields itself to a systematic order of enquiry. Arming himself with the available facts from the basic researcher, the applied researcher searches the known to discover yet unknown facts or to improve upon the existing state of knowledge.

Finally, it is necessary to note that when we talk of original research, we are referring to research that is not based on a synthesis of previous investigations. It is considered a primary source, the purpose being to produce new knowledge. Unlike applied research, which may present existing knowledge in a novel or innovative form, original research develops from an original idea.

Normative Research and the Scientific Method

There are two major methods of research: normative research and the scientific method. Normative research is based entirely on the impressionistic observations of the investigator. Usually, the investigator applying the normative method begins with the stated possible conclusion, after which he goes on to scout for possible evidence to support the conclusion. As a result, normative research is descriptive in nature and seeks to establish norms, standards, and guidelines necessary for the study of a phenomenon. It can also employ quantitative methods to collect data or normative samples. Though it establishes benchmarks, normative research may have its own limitations, especially in terms of generality.

The scientific method is considered the most reliable approach to research. This is because it operates on the belief that the world is constructed in complex chains of causal relationships which can be totally discerned through systematic investigation. This belief led scientists to evolve an organized system of discovering causal relationships, and appropriate methods of testing the accuracy of the conclusions reached because it involves observations, formulation of hypotheses, and diligent testing of the hypothesis, the application of experiments and appropriate data collection and analysis. As a result, it involves the processes of design and conduct of experiments, analysis, drawing conclusions and appropriate communication of those conclusions. Its major principles are objectivity, empiricism, and open design tests. The ultimate aim is to develop new knowledge.

The term *scientific method,* therefore, does not imply a research method peculiar to the sciences. It means a systematic method of investigation aimed at the solution to a problem. Since the scientific method constitutes stating the research question, collecting relevant data, and drawing pertinent conclusions from the evidence collected and analyzed, five major steps are considered necessary in scientific research.

1. Identifying an event to be investigated;
2. Gathering information on the event or events;
3. Developing a theory or hypothesis to explain the event;
4. Testing the theory or hypothesis through experimentation;
5. Evaluating the theory or hypothesis.

The Purpose of Research

The purpose of research is to investigate an area of scholarship and put the results of such investigation carefully and systematically into written form. It is important that the researcher takes good care of what he says and the way he says it because these are taken into consideration in evaluating the final product. The research product should be lucid and coherent. Personal knowledge of the area is not enough. The researcher needs to investigate pertinent, relevant, and related sources in order to discover new information.

Since it involves active learning, research writing exposes the researcher to many areas of knowledge: the use of the library, methods of data collection and analysis, knowledge of accepted documentation styles, the mechanics of research and the importance of logical thinking. Research also teaches the investigator the method of organization, analysis, and lucid imagination. In the end, the researcher gains significant knowledge on the subject of investigation and transmits that knowledge to the reader in coherent prose.

The final product of research should not be a massive collection of the opinions of other people but a carefully and logically constructed presentation which documents original ideas and which relies on a multitude of sources for clarification and verification. A good researcher should have his own problem to investigate, organize information in such a way that the reader has a new insight into the subject of investigation, and present his own unique conclusions.

Qualities of a Good Researcher

A good researcher must be a curious person, a person whose curiosity causes him to engage in an investigation into an unknown phenomenon in order to establish its existence. It is this curiosity that causes him to attempt to try out a new technique or evolve methods of interpreting an existing phenomenon.

Secondly, a good researcher must be a voracious reader. He must develop an interest in reading because it is through reading that a lacuna in knowledge can be detected.

Finally, a good researcher must be a skeptic. He must doubt whatever he reads and read whatever he doubts. It is this doubt that causes him to attempt to establish its veracity or debunk its authenticity. As Richard D. Altick puts it,

To be a good researcher, one must be a thoroughgoing skeptic. Though in his personal relations, he may be the most benevolent and trusting of men, professionally, he must cultivate a low opinion of the human capacity for truth and accuracy – beginning with his own. The well-spring of wisdom in research …… is self-knowledge (23),

A good researcher should, therefore, know how to think logically, how to organize effectively, how to appropriately discriminate between useful and useless information, and how to document properly.

Two

SELECTING A RESEARCH TOPIC

*Choosing a topic is like choosing a room mate; it is essential
to make sure that you can live with your choice*

-Michael Meyer

*When you stop learning, stop listening, stop looking and asking questions,
always new questions, then it is time to die.*

-Lillian Smith

The selection of a research topic is very crucial to the success of the investigation as a whole. It is the first serious decision to be taken by the researcher because it serves as a scholarly guide throughout the period of the research. Appropriate selection of a research topic is the necessary first step towards the successful execution of a research project. Therefore, care should be exercised in selecting a research topic. To select an ideal topic, the researcher should consider the following points:

The Researcher's Interest

The researcher should select a topic that is capable of arousing his interest and curiosity. Research involves a large amount of investigation and the examination of relevant and related sources. If the researcher is interested and curious enough about the topic selected, he will happily search all available sources and hence make pertinent and worthwhile conclusions. A worthwhile research must develop naturally out of simple curiosity. It must be fed imagination, ingenuity, creativity, improvisation, and dedicated effort.

Availability of Research Materials

Before selecting a topic, the researcher must ensure that the materials necessary for the completion of the study are available in the institution where the research is to be undertaken, or at least in its environs. If the materials are not within the reach of the researcher, the results of the research may not be authentic because the researcher may not have availed himself of the opportunity to examine the maze of available material in the area of investigation.

To ameliorate this problem, the researcher should scout for sources in other places. University libraries and research centres have inter-library loan facilities, and the researcher should take advantage of such facilities in the execution of the research.

Researcher's Knowledge of the Topic

The researcher should avoid a topic where he has a mere rudimentary understanding of the subject of investigation. It is true that research is an enquiry into the unknown, but the enquiry becomes tedious if the researcher lacks basic knowledge of the topic being investigated.

Subjective/Controversial Topics

It is not advisable for a researcher to engage in a subjective or controversial topic unless he is forced to do so. In selecting such a topic, the researcher must ensure that the topic should be treated with objectivity and that the final conclusions should not be subjective. Similarly, he should ensure that the topic selected is not as controversial as to yield shades of argument in his reasoned conclusion.

If the researcher must investigate an inflammatory of controversial topic, he should comply candidly with appropriate TECHNIQUE regarding researches of this nature. Specifically, he should try to be intellectually honest and avoid bigoted and propagandistic sources in his selection of material or research. He should not deliberately omit relevant evidence and must avoid the presentation of half-truths or generalizations that are not clearly substantiated. And finally, he should weigh collected evidence objectively and rationally.

Manageability of the Topic

The researcher should select a topic that is appropriate for the particular research being undertaken, whether it is a term paper, a thesis or a dissertation. Some topics are so broad that they cannot be effectively managed in a standard research work. Such topics should be shifted and narrowed down until they become manageable and amenable to research.

Invariably, some topics are so narrow that the researcher becomes hungry for information and begins to add extraneous material to beef up the work. Such topics should be avoided by a serious researcher.

Time Factor

The time for the submission of the final research report should be taken into consideration in the selection of the research topic. Research undertaken for the Bachelor's or Master's degree may be completed within an academic session, while doctoral dissertations take a much longer period. The researcher must ensure that the study must be completed within the specified time. In this regard, he should be certain that the subject of investigation is such that it can be finished within the time proposed. If he is in doubt, he should choose another subject in order to avoid the possibility of having to spend more time on the project than is permissible.

Topics to be Avoided

These six points have indirectly covered topics to be avoided in the selection of a research topic. In addition, it is necessary to state that the researcher should avoid topics that can be developed from the researcher's own personal experience. It is important to select a topic on which conclusions can be drawn from a variety of sources, not merely from a single outside source or the researcher's own personal experience.

Finally, the researcher should avoid topics that have been overworked unless he has tangible and innovative information that would make it more inventive and interesting to the reader. It is this originality that makes the work significant and engaging.

Narrowing Down the Topic

The danger of handling broad topics is that the researcher faces the problem of selection. With the avalanche of information on very broad topics he may be overwhelmed with so much information that he finds it difficult to effectively do justice to the topic. It is also possible for the researcher to omit pertinent material, which could ultimately create a lacuna in the final conclusion.

To arrest this problem the researcher should narrow down the topic to make it suitable and amenable to a thesis or dissertation situation. To achieve this, he should be guided by common sense as well as the availability of research materials. It is, therefore, necessary for the researcher to sift the topic rigorously, evaluating and experimenting with it until it becomes appropriate to the particular research being undertaken. The purpose of the research should also be taken into consideration in narrowing down the topic.

If the researcher has chosen a broad subject, he should narrow it down to a particular area of the subject and finally to a manageable sequence. For instance, a researcher in the area of Theatre and Film Studies may choose Dramatic Theory and Criticism as the broad area of investigation. From this broad area, he narrows it down to a particular area of criticism like Theatre of the Absurd. This is still not manageable. He now recognizes that absurdism cannot be discussed without absurd plays for explanation. He may finally settle for the topic: "Manifestations of Absurdism in the plays of Tewfik Al-Hakim". Note that the choice is not confined to the theory of absurdism. The researcher can choose another area of Dramatic Theory and Criticism, or even another playwright or combination of playwrights whose plays are considered as belonging to the theory of absurdism, to investigate.

A researcher in Oral literature, for instance, may decide to research on Igbo mythology as a broad area. He then narrows it down to the Ojadili myth, and finally to a researchable topic which may deal with any area of the myth. He may eventually settle for the title "Narrative Techniques in Ojadili".

Now, let us take the case of a student of Physics. He narrowed the research area down to Astronomy and still needs to engage in final narrowing to create a researchable topic. He may come up with a title like "Facts about Planets as provided by Space Travel". Notice that writing on facts about planets generally will be a monster-sized topic, hence the focus on facts provided by space travel.

An engineering scholar, on the other hand, may decide to focus his research on the area of automobiles. He may decide on a comparative study, and his final narrowing may be stated as follows: "Three types of Early Automobiles: A Comparative Study".

One more example will be necessary. A student in the general area of Music has too many areas to narrow his topic down to. If, for instance, he chooses to study the matter and manner of lyrics in musical compositions, he still needs to narrow it down to a manageable, researchable topic. He may arrive at the title: "Social Commentary in the music of Fela Anikulapo-Kuti.

The examples are endless. The most important thing is that the idea begins from a broad area to a particular area of the discipline and finally terminates with the identification of a researchable topic.

The researcher should remember that some exploratory reading on the subject of investigation is necessary before focusing on the final topic of the research.

Developing a Thesis

It is necessary to develop a thesis after narrowing down the selected topic. A thesis is the central idea of the research topic. It summarizes the researcher's approach to the topic and provides the rationale for the investigation.

At this time in the research process, what the researcher has is the working thesis, which could be revised and focus more on the purpose of the research, especially after he has started work on the topic.

The research thesis takes the form of a declarative statement and should not be in question form, though a question may yield the statement so declared. The definition of the central idea determines the evidence that should be included in the research report.

Since the thesis statement shows both the purpose of the study and the approach to be used in writing the final report, it should reveal the focus of the study as well as determine what is to be proven in the research report.

Three

GATHERING INFORMATION

Research can range all the way from simple fact-digging to the most obtuse speculations....

-Legget, Mead and Charvat.

Knowledge is of two kinds. We know a subject ourselves or we know where we can find information upon it.

-Samuel Johnson

The Development of Writing

The human need to receive and process information in order to communicate and preserve knowledge started from the fossil print carved indelibly in rock and transited to the computer printout, which is contemporary and electronically operated. Information processing started with oral tradition, during which time people communicated through the spoken word by passing information orally from generation to generation. Limitations of memory and distance militated against this form of information transmission, which was mainly encapsulated in songs, folklore, stories and poetry. To ameliorate this, a system of mnemonic devices was used for the communication and storage of records before the development of writing.

Writing developed from pictures which depicted the spoken word before the advent of the alphabet. This development looks at three distinct stages: the *pictographic,* the *ideographic,* and the *phonetic.* The pictographic depicted pictures painted on natural surfaces, while the ideographic constituted drawings representing an idea. Phonetic writing, a representation of linguistic elements, also followed three stages of development – the *word symbol,* the *syllabic* and the *alphabetic.*

The main system of writing that preceded the alphabetic was invented by the Sumerians of Southern Mesopotamia. Known as Cuneiform, this style of writing started in 5000 BC. It shifted from the ideographic to the phonetic in 3000 BC. Hieroglyphic, another form of writing, was developed by the Egyptians in 4000 BC. It also developed by passing from the ideographic to the phonetic.

Writing faced a lot of metamorphosis when it began to spread to different cultures. For instance, the Phonecians borrowed from the Egyptians, and the Greeks borrowed from the Phoenicians, and this led to the emergence of the first system of vowel sounds. The Roman alphabet, the progenitor of the English alphabet, originated from Etrusca and Greece and was marked by the reduction of the alphabet to twenty-three letters. It spread through Europe unchanged, except for the addition of three new letters as well as changes in the form of the script.

The Development of the Library

The most important factor in the processing of information is information storage. With the records now in written form, the need for their preservation became a necessity, and the evolution of the library as a storehouse for the accumulation, organization and transmission of knowledge became imperative.

The word library comes from the word *liber,* which means *book.* The Greeks and credited with the evolution of the first public library, which was established in Athens in 500 BC. The Greek philosopher Aristotle also founded a library in the Lyceum and this was considered the most extensive collection of the period until the collection was moved to Rome in 88 BC after the Roman invasion of Greece by the Vandals. Emperor Augustus eventually built the first Roman public library in 33 BC, while Emperor Trajan built the magnificent Ulpiana library in 98 AD. By 476 AD, when the Vandals invaded Rome, there were twenty-six public libraries in Greece, all of which were either destroyed or looted.

The Use of the Library in Research

The first place the researcher goes to gather research information is the library. The researcher needs to familiarize himself with the use of this library in order to effectively make use of its facilities. Basically, he should know the utility of the following parts of the library – **the circulation desk**, which is where library books are checked out; the **reference section,** which contains reference books like Encyclopedias, Almanacs, Handbooks, Dictionaries, Bibliographies and Periodical indexes; the ***card catalogue***, which contains an alphabetical listing of all the books in the library; *the stacks,* which are bookshelves where the books are kept; the *reserve room* which contains the books temporarily removed from the shelves and reserved for a particular use and should not be checked out of the library, the **serials section**, which house journals and periodical; and the **newspaper racks,** the Xerox room and the **typing room**. In recent times the typing room is now being faced out in favour of the computer room.

A serious researcher should not hesitate to request for assistance from library staff because they are usually willing to help with the solution of any problems encountered in the library.

Library Classification Systems

The classification systems of libraries have become so complex that they differ from library to library. However, the major classification systems used in major libraries are the *Dewey Decimal System* and the *Library of Congress System*. The researcher needs to be familiar with the classification system of the library being used to enable him execute the research without major problems.

Finding Information

The first step in gathering information is to get general background material on the topic of investigation. To achieve this, it is beneficial for the researcher to begin his investigation in the reference room. He should consult reference sources in order to get a general overview of the topic of investigation. Of immense use of the researcher are the Encyclopedia, and other reference sources. Similarly, the researcher should check the card catalogue under the subject heading for pertinent information on appropriate sources of information on the subject of y the investigation.

The reference room also contains periodical indexes, which list articles published in periodicals. These indexes are very valuable sources of information and should, on no account, be ignored by a serious researcher. Some journals publish cumulative indexes, which are sometimes incorporated into a particular volume of the journal. This gives a listing of articles published in previous issues of the journal.

The Domino Theory

It is necessary for the researcher to know the reference work is limited to giving general background information on the area of investigation. The importance of reference works is governed by the domino theory. Specifically, the domino theory refers to the practice where one source of research information leads the researcher to another source or even to a multitude of sources. An article will lead the researcher to a book, a journal, or a magazine by references, suggestions for further reading, or by a listing of select bibliography of sources in the research area. This is why documentation is an important part of the research process.

Assembling a Working Bibliography

A working bibliography is a preliminary list of sources that will be used in the execution of the research. The sources include encyclopedias, books, journal articles, scholarly reviews, computer databases and information on microform.

Index cards are recommended for use in compiling the working bibliography, but the researcher is free to use any method he considers appropriate. Information in the bibliography card must include the following: the library call number of the book; the full name(s) of the author(s); the exact title of the book or article; and publication information comprising the publisher, place and date of publication.

If the source is a scholarly article, the exact name of the journal, the date of publication, the volume number, and the inclusive page numbers of the article should be stated. If it is a reference work, the name of the source, the volume number, the title of the material, the name of the author (if stated), and the library call number of the reference work should be clearly stated. It will be valuable to the researcher if each entry is followed by a brief note on the contents of the source and, if possible, the likely usefulness of the source in the research.

Checking the Usefulness of a Book

It is important for the researcher to evaluate the sources identified in order to ensure their usefulness in the execution of the research being undertaken. To achieve this, he needs to know the parts of a book since each part contributes to the usefulness of the book. A book is made up of the following sections: the *preliminary pages,* the main *text,* and the *auxiliary or reference section.*

Every book is preceded by preliminary pages. These include the half-page title, the title page, the copyright information, the preface, table of contents, list of illustrations and the introduction. The title page is the authoritative source of information on documentation. It contains the title, the sub-title, the author's name (or that of the edition, illustrator or translator), and copyright information.

The preface is a brief essay stating the special features of the study. It includes the purpose of the work, the scope and limitations of the study, and acknowledgments. The introduction is a succinct essay stating the general background of the subject of investigation. It also makes preliminary statements leading to the contents of the book.

The text is the main body of the book and houses the required information on the subject of investigation. It is usually divided into chapters and/or parts. The auxiliary or reference section contains materials inserted at the end of the study to aid readers and other researchers in obtaining pertinent information about the book. They usually include the glossary, which is a list of definitions and technical terms used in the book; the eppendiz, which supplies supplementary materials like maps and tables; the bibliography, which is a documentation of books, articles and other sources which aided the author in writing the book. Sometimes, the bibliography is annotated. Finally, this section contains the book's index, which is an alphabetical list of subjects discussed in the book. This is usually matched with the pages where the subjects appear in the book.

Evaluating Research Sources

The relevance and reliability of the sources listed in the working bibliography should be ascertained before it is considered as an acceptable source of material for the study. First, the sources should be categorized into primary and secondary sources. Primary sources are the ones that provide original information on the research topic, while secondary sources are usually in the form of comments and interpretations, which add color to the primary sources.

The first point to be taken into consideration in the evaluation of research sources is the currency of the source. Here, the pertinent question is: is this source up-to-date? An up-to-date source usually gives a historical overview of previous studies through its review of literature and reference list. It is a known fact that the more recent a book, the more up-to-date the contents, though there is a possibility of having a recent book without up-to-date information. Older publications may be incomplete or inaccurate in reaching a final conclusion because the information contained in them may have been debunked in more recent publications.

The credibility of the source is also very important. The researcher should examine the author of the material in order to ascertain his credibility. He should find out if the author is an expert in the area, a trained researcher, or a prejudiced mind.

The nature of the source is another factor to be taken into consideration in the evaluation. The fact that a book is published does not ensure its accuracy as a research source. The researcher should find out who sponsored the publication or if the author is merely defending a particular point of view. Books published by reputable publishers are preferable to those published (or even printed) by the authors themselves. The status of the publisher should, therefore, be taken into consideration in evaluating the sources. It is also important to examine the sufficiency of the source by checking whether the publication reflects scholarship based on primary sources. Finally, a review of the source should not be neglected.

It is important to discern what reviewers think about the source since reputable journals select reviewers from scholars who have spent years of solid research on the subject being reviewed. Their evaluation may help the researcher in determining the relevant contribution of the source of the study.

Selecting sources

The researcher does not need to read every book or article written on the subject before deciding on its suitability for the study. In fact, he seldom had enough time to do so, even if he wanted to. A good researcher determines the suitability of is source through a number of methods. First, it is necessary to skim through the book or article to avoid spending unnecessary time in the determination of the utility of the book.

Skimming through a book should be a creative activity. The preface should be read, and the introduction should be glanced through in order to capture the main ideas of the book. The table of contents should also be carefully scrutinized since it gives the researcher an overview of the general topics covered in the book.

While skimming through a scholarly article, the researcher needs to read the opening paragraph of the article before forming his opinion on the usefulness of the source. This is because the author's thesis is usually stated in the first or second paragraph of the essay. Similarly, the concluding paragraph should be perused so as to have an idea of the author's conclusion as well as how useful such conclusion promises to be in the execution of the extant research.

The next important act is to look up the subject of investigation in the book's index. The number of pages allotted to the subject in the book will help the researcher in determining the usefulness of the source of the extant research. If the book covers just a few pages on the subject of investigation, it may not be deemed useful as a primary source.

Internet Sources

Internet means an Interconnectivity network. In the contemporary global society, the evolution of the Internet as an indispensable research tool should not be ignored by any serious researcher. Apart from being an aid to research, the Internet is also an invaluable communication tool. As a result, there is an avalanche of information on the Internet which would be useful to the researcher. They vary in length, quality and currency. The researcher is, therefore, required to be very discriminatory in the choice of Internet materials to use and cite in a research report.

To evaluate the validity and reliability of information obtained from the Internet, the following factors should be taken into consideration:

a) Ensure that the material is posted by a recognized authority in the area of investigation. The researcher should find out who is responsible for posting the information. Is he a known expert in the field or a self-proclaimed expert? It is important to note that websites of government agencies (those that end in .gov), as well as educational institutions (the ones that end in .edu), have more credibility and reliability than organizational sites (those that end in .org) and commercial sites (those that end in .com).

b) Check the nature of the information. Evaluate its scope and source in order to discern whether it presents facts or mere opinions. If, in your opinion, the quality of information in the source is defective, discard it and look for other sources.

c) Evaluate the accuracy of the posted information. Can the information contained therein be corroborated with information in other authoritative print sources? If you doubt the accuracy of the posted material, discard it.

d) Examine the information carefully to ensure that it is objective and not self-opinionated or biased. As with printed sources, avoid materials whose objectivity is in doubt or one that is merely defending a point of view. (e) Check when the information was posted and assess how recently it has been updated. To ensure the currency of the Internet source, check the date of the last upgrade. This is usually listed at the bottom of the Web site's home page. If there is no date, that is not a good sign. Such sources should be used with care and caution.

Advantages and Disadvantages of the Internet

Internet search has an avalanche of advantages and disadvantages for the researcher. The advantages include the following: having multiple sources and Web pages available to the researcher, ease and speed in retrieving research material from all parts of the world, ability to chat with other scholars in the area whose abode may be distant from the researcher's place of domicile and the luxury of personal access to information from the home or library.

The disadvantages include the decentralization and disorganization of Internet information. Because of the number of people using the Internet for all kinds of purposes, the exact source may be difficult to find, and the researcher could spend valuable time browsing endlessly from one site to another without obtaining the required information. If the site is busy, waiting for the source to download can be wearisome and exasperating. Finally, Internet sources may be devoid of accuracy and reliability.

Search Engines

Search engines are services that render invaluable services like indexing, organizing, rating and reviewing Web sites that focus on a multiplicity of information. The researcher should try different search engines if he experiences any difficulty in obtaining the required information from one engine. The following represent, in alphabetical order, the major search engines available to the Internet researcher:

1. *Altavista* - This is a gigantic engine which indexes about one hundred and fifty million Web pages. This includes information in foreign languages from ten nations.

2. ***Excite*** - This uses software to catalogue Web sites.

3. ***Google***-This search engine searches nearly four billion Websites. Its results are produced in order of popularity, which is determined by the number of links from other standard sites. Google sites include sites from ten non-English speaking countries.

4. ***Hot Bot*** - This engine indexes over one hundred and twenty million Web sites. These indexes are searched by date, media, type, language, or location.

5. ***Infoseek***- This is a search engine that uses software and people to review Web sites. Its main advantage is that it provides a special directory of sites indicated by word order. Its emphasis is on news.

6. ***Lycos*** - This is similar to Excite and Infoseek and indexes nearly sixty million Web sites using software and people.

7. ***Yahoo*** - This is an enormous global search engine which uses software and people to list and evaluate sites.

The researcher can also link to universities around the world. The home page will direct the researcher to appropriate links in the institutions where research activities could be listed.

Four

THE RESEARCH OUTLINE

SION

You know when you think about writing a book, you think it is overwhelming. But, actually, you break it down into tiny little tasks any moron could do.

- **Annie Dillard.**

Do not follow where the path may lead. Go instead where there is no path and leave a trail.

- **Anon**

Meaning

The outline is a listing of topics meant to be covered in a research project. It is written in an orderly manner and serves as a reminder to the writer (or even the reader) of important information covered in the paper and the order in which they have been dealt with. The outline varies in complexity, size and style and serves as a tool for the convenience of both the writer and the reader.

The purpose of the outline is to avoid the possibility of straying from the point. It helps the writer to avoid the danger of skimping on one topic and overdeveloping or ignoring the other. To the reader the outline serves as a detailed and comprehensive table of contents which itemizes the items covered in the study. Because of the importance of the outline in the research process, a good researcher spends more time planning the work than in the actual writing. A detailed, polished outline guides the researcher faithfully to the finished product.

Elements of the Outline

In writing the outline, the researcher should ensure that the major topics are broad enough to contain the subject of investigation. Second, the outline entries should be specific enough that each topic can be discussed in detail. Third, the outline should be successively partitioned in such a way that each successive level is a division of the level immediately preceding it. Fourth, it is necessary to use a logical notation and consistent format in order to show the subordination of some parts of the topic to others. Finally, the researcher should ensure that all sections and sub-sections of the outline are ordered, capitalized, lettered, numbered and indented to show the relationship between the parts of the outline on the one hand and the overall discussion on the other.

Types of Outlines

There are three main types of outlines: the topic outline, the sentence outline, and the paragraph outline. Consistency is important in designing an outline so that these types are not mixed together or absurdly combined.

In the topic outline, each entry is worded as a phrase. The subjects are then broken into sub-headings. The sentence outline uses a complete sentence for each entry. These sentences are more effective if they are declarative sentences.

Because the entries in a sentence outline are detailed, they provide the writer with a good overview of the study.

In the paragraph outline, entries are recorded as a complete paragraph. This provides a condensed version of the paper and is very valuable to the beginning researcher since it enables him to summarize sections of the study in whole paragraphs.

Composing the Outline

It is necessary to remember that the outline is a tool for the writer's convenience. Therefore, a significant amount of reading is supposed to have taken place before a formal outline is composed. After this extensive reading, the researcher should write the statement of purpose. This states specifically what is required to be accomplished in the study.

The next important step to take in the composition of an outline is brainstorming. The purpose of brainstorming is to get ideas down on paper. Think about the subject critically and write down every idea that comes to mind. Ensure that there are enough concrete details to work with.

The brainstorming technique is a way of tackling a research project effectively from all sides. For this to be effective, the researcher should strive for quality, making sure to combine and improve ideas as the work progresses.

It is expedient to sift through the brainstorming list carefully and organize the relevant major topics from the list in a logical sequence. The stated purpose should be borne in mind during this process. After this exercise, the research should produce a working outline which is an informal guide to the study.

The next necessary step is to collect all the relevant data needed for the execution of the research. It is necessary to use the rough or informal outline as a guide for data collection. If the data suggests the inclusion of additional topics, the working outline should be reworked accordingly.

Choice of Outline

It is clear from the foregoing that the researcher should have done enough work on the research topic before developing an outline. The formal outline is not merely a list of what the researcher intends to do but a blueprint of how he intends to do it. As a result, the outline serves as scaffolding for the research report. The rough draft becomes a transcription and development of the outline.

Sometimes, the researcher worries about the kind of outline to use. While beginning researchers may find the sentence outline more beneficial to their purposes, more experienced researchers use the topic outline. The two methods yield a number of advantages to the researcher. While the sentence outline enables the beginning researcher to fill in the blanks and insert transitions and connectives in the skeleton in order to develop the full essay, the topic outline enables the experienced researcher to indulge in comprehensive intellectual argument in the development of the topic outlined.

General Model of an Outline

Whatever the kind of outline used, it is necessary to develop the outline from a model. The following will serve as a guide to the researcher.

1: INTRODUCTION

(a) The introduction should contain the statement of the problem, the definition, history and significance of the subject of investigation.

(b) Statement of Purpose;

(c) Audience information on the topic - this should be in the form of a brief review of scholarship aimed at informing the reader of the present state of research in the area. The review of the scholarship eventually forms a separate chapter during the final report.

(d) Information sources: this should include research methods and materials.

(e) Working definitions this is necessary only when there are peculiar terms or concepts to be defined.

(f) Limitations of the research, if any.

(g) Scope of coverage (or a succinct statement on the organization of the rest of the chapters of the study.

II: THE BODY OF THE REPORT

This represents the component parts of the subject and should be divided into sub-sections as appropriate. These sub-sections may, in turn, constitute the chapters as necessary. The following method is recommended for the body of the study.

A. First Major Topic

   1. First sub-topic of A
   2. Second sub-topic of A
        a. First sub-topic of 2
        b. Second sub-topic of 2

This development should continue as much as possible, depending on the nature of the research. The sub-divisions should go on as far as is necessary. The major topics should also be carried on as far as necessary because they will ultimately constitute the chapters of the report.

III: CONCLUSION

This is the section where everything is tied together. Since it wraps up the report, it may be in the form of a summary of information contained in the report. It may also contain recommendations and proposals based on the findings in the body of the report.

Decimal Notation of the Outline

Decimal notation is now a very popular outline pattern in many academic areas. This kind of outline is based on the decimal accounting system and gives the researcher the opportunity to add sub-divisions infinitely by merely adding another decimal place. Here is an example of a general pattern of notation in decimal form.

Topic of Study: Igbo Masquerade Drama

1.0 Masquerading in Igboland

1.1 Origin Organization and Membership

      1.2.1 Initiation of Members

1.3 Categories of Masquerades

      1.3.1 Achikwu

      1.3.2 Onyekuteredike

1.3.3 Ichoku

2.0 A typical Masquerade Display

    2.1 The Rehearsal Period

    2.2 The Performance Proper

    2.2.1 The Arena

    2.2.2 The Opening Glee

    2,2,3 Dramatic Enactments

The additions should continue until all the points are covered. Each major Arabic numeral may eventually constitute a chapter in the report.

Generic Method

Hereunder is the general method of developing the decimal notation outline:

(a) Use Roman numerals for major areas

(b) Use capital letters for major topics

(c) Use Arabic numerals for sub-topics

(d) Use lowercase letters for further divisions as appropriate.

Revision Checklist

The quality of the outline is very important in the research process. To ensure that the quality of the outline is in deed high, the following checklist is recommended.

1. Is the outline broad enough to encompass the topic of investigation?
2. Are the sub-divisions specific enough to represent all major and minor points?
3. Should some minor points be changed to major points, or vice versa?
4. Is the format consistent?
5. Is every item placed in the best logical location?
6. Are all the necessary topics and sub-topics represented?
7. Is the outline clear and easy to follow?
8. Is the system of notation as logical as necessary?

Five

THE RESEARCH PROPOSAL

We all know what light is, But it is not easy to tell what it is.

- James Bosswell

You can write about anything, and if you write well enough, even the reader with no intrinsic interest in the subject will become involved.

- **Tracy Kidder.**

The presentation of a research proposal is a very important step in the research process. In many research projects, especially those dealing with postgraduate degrees, the approval of the topic is contingent upon the submission of an acceptable research proposal. Apart from providing a basis for the evaluation of the matter and manner of the proposed study, the proposal provides the researcher with a systematic plan or procedure for the execution of the research.

Classification of Scholarly Activities

It is necessary for the researcher to recognize that scholarly activities are varied in a number of ways. Whether it is a description of scientific experiments, survey of opinion or broad generalizations based on evidence, scholarly activities are generally classified into three types: fact-finding, critical interpretation and the final analytical discourse. It is necessary for the researcher to take this into consideration in the preparation of a research proposal.

Characteristics of Critical Thinking

Critical thinking involves the skill of asking appropriate questions as well as the ability to control one's mental activities. It is a process of testing assertions and arguments to determine their veracity. It encompasses the search for answers, conscious evaluation, and a quest whose major technique is asking probing questions, which are ultimately used to analyze issues. It is devoid of feeling since feeling is subjective and reflects sentiments and emotion.

A researcher is considered a critical thinker when he is honest with his search, recognizes his limitations, and watches out for his own possible errors. He strives for a comprehensive understanding of the subject of the investigation, which he approaches with curiosity and excitement. A critical thinker bases his conclusions or judgement on evidence rather than personal feelings and should not make conclusions until he has sufficient evidence to work with. He should read voraciously, listen attentively, even when in disagreement with another opinion, exercise fair-mindedness and restraint, and always resist from endorsing an idea until it has been tested and confirmed.

Scholars reject uncritical thinking because the uncritical thinker is devoid of the propensity for research and a pretender to knowledge because he pretends to know more than he does. He ignores, or is unaware of, his limitations, is self-opinionated and impatient, and bases his conclusions on first impressions and instinctive reactions. Because he is so preoccupied with his own views, opinions, and feelings, the uncritical thinker shuns balanced judgment.

Whether it is a description of scientific experiments, a survey of opinion or broad generalizations based on evidence, critical thinking involves three basic activities: Investigation, Interpretation, and Judgement or Conclusion.

Investigation (Fact Finding)

This is one of the first steps a serious researcher engages in during the research process. It is the process of looking for evidence or data that are both relevant and sufficient enough to be subjected to appropriate interpretation with the aim of reaching appropriate conclusions.

There are different kinds of evidence, and the most important ones are personal experiences, published and unpublished works, eyewitness accounts, expert opinions, survey, statistics, experiments, observations (formal and participant), and research reviews.

Evidence is considered sufficient when its quality and quantity permit conclusions to be reached with certainty. In a journal article, the conclusion may appear immediately after the introduction or in the conclusion. In a book, the conclusion may appear in the first, second, or last chapter. Expressions like Consequently, Therefore, Thus, So indicate conclusions.

Critical Interpretation

The term critical interpretation refers to the art of critical evaluation of the facts collected. It is the process of deciding the meaning of the evidence obtained during the process of fact-finding.

It is necessary to note that intellectual criticism is not merely the process of finding faults but a systematic method of assessing the positive and negative aspects of a material in order to arrive at objective conclusions. Subjecting the facts to critical interpretation, not mere interpretation, is paramount. Though critical interpretation is considered the scholarly forte of research in the Humanities, the fact still remains that in all areas of research, critical interpretation is indispensable.

During the process of critical interpretation, the researcher should be guided by perspicacity and logic. In this way the strengths and weaknesses of the facts as means of answering the research question will be ascertained. To ensure effectiveness, the arguments advanced in critical interpretation must be in tandem with known principles in the area of investigation and the conclusions reached should derive logically from the fact being interpreted. The overall outcome of the interpretation is the reasoned opinion of the researcher and should be supported by evidence and logic.

Final Conclusion or Judgement

Judgement is the act of reaching a conclusion based on a scrupulous and exhaustive examination of the evidence and the attendant careful reasoning. The final judgement represents what eventually results from both fact-finding and critical interpretation. An appropriate research effort consists of a problem to be solved, data collected, careful analysis and critical interpretation of the evidence leading to a definite solution or answer to the question posed by the problem identified by the researcher.

A good researcher should endeavour to present a balanced view of the issue under discussion. To obtain a balanced view, the astute researcher should reflect all the intricacies and complexities of the issue.

The researcher should always have these characteristics and classifications in mind while preparing a research proposal because the proposal is comparable to an architectural blueprint and, therefore, indispensable in the research process. Any worthwhile research product inevitably results from a well. Designed research proposal.

Preliminary Statements

The first step in the preparation of a research proposal is to make copious preliminary statements on the general purpose of the investigation. This represents the statement of the problem and should be designed either in question form or in the nature of a declarative statement. The problem must be limited in scope in order to make it possible for the researcher to reach a definite conclusion from it. This should be followed by a declarative statement indicating the logic of the investigation. The aim is to provide the rationale which underlies the proposal as well as a brief statement on the theoretical framework of the study.

The Hypothesis

A hypothesis is an educated guess or a hunch and is designed as a tentative answer to a question. It is eventually subjected to verification for confirmation or disconfirmation. It is advisable for the researcher to formulate one major hypothesis and some minor ones. It is important to note that the hypotheses should be stated with absolute care because the rest of the proposal derives from them. A good hypothesis should be reasonable, consistent with known facts or theories, and be stated in such a way as to yield to tests regarding its probability. A description of the methods to be used in testing the hypotheses may be very useful.

The major hypothesis can also be stated in a negative or null form. This is described as a null hypothesis. It is necessary to state, in the final analysis, that a good researcher should formulate the hypothesis before the actual data collection in order to ensure an unbiased investigation.

Significance of the Problem

Many research projects, especially those carried out by students at both undergraduate and postgraduate levels, are efforts at trivial or superficial investigation. Some of them present theories without facts which, in the words of Robert Dubin, should more appropriately be labeled "theology". Much of the research paraded as original or significant is either borrowed or derived and may stand firm when subjected to critical analysis. Many theses and dissertations written in universities can hardly stand at a level above the requirements of the prescribed degree programme. This is why it is necessary to state the significance of the proposed research.

Definitions, Assumptions and Limitations

The research should give a succinct definition of all terms that could be confusing or yield different kinds of meanings to the reader. This will help to show exactly the meaning attached to the term in the extant research. The purpose of this definition is to ensure the establishment of a frame of reference with which the problem will be handled in the study. The researcher also needs to state the assumptions and limitations of the research with significant honesty in order to avoid the danger of over-generalization.

A Brief Review of Related Literature

There is a need to provide a brief summary of major research previously concluded in the area of investigation. This will pave the way for a more comprehensive review of scholarship which will ultimately occupy a chapter in the proposed study. This brief review of related literature stands as an assurance that the researcher is familiar with the state of the research in the area of investigation. If possible, the researcher should conclude with a succinct statement showing the areas of agreement and disagreement in the studies reviewed. This review is not merely an enumeration of previous studies in the area. It should be used to develop the background and logic of the proposed research and thus establish the need for the present study.

Theoretical Framework

It is necessary to succinctly discuss the concept of the theoretical framework here because of its importance in the research process especially at the postgraduate level. Usually, a researcher presenting a research proposal is required to construct a theoretical framework which will ultimately serve as a guide to the study, particularly with regard to the determination of the things to be measured and the data necessary for the achievement of desired results.

Some people have the erroneous belief that the development of a theoretical framework is not necessary in some academic areas. They tend to support this falsehood by citing the utility of the theoretical framework in deductive and theory-testing investigations. But the point is that theoretical framework, as a research concept, does not involve the creation of theories.

Theory, etymologically speaking, is derived from the Greek word theoria meaning speculation through contemplation. Such speculation should be stated in such a way that renders it verifiable through investigative study. While theory may involve the analysis of related concepts, theoretical or conceptual framework unites interrelated ideas.

Simply put theoretical framework involves stating the structure of the research concept and how this structure will be developed in the study. It is also appropriate to describe it as a conceptual framework because it brings the interrelated theories involved in the research question into one monolithic entity. Because a researcher cultivates a multitude of interrelated concepts in order to give them a new interpretation, a theoretical or conceptual framework synthesizes these concepts in order to explain their interrelationship. Whether or not a thesis or dissertation contains a theory, it will obviously contain a concept or series of concepts that need to be explained and ranked in relation to the main research question.

Theoretical framework has a close affinity with a review of scholarship. As will be discussed in the next chapter, the review is not a listing of studies carried out in the area of investigation but an analysis of previous studies which the researcher considers crucial in substantiating his ideas or concepts. A careful documentation of these studies clearly steers the reader to the researcher's theoretical or conceptual framework. A lot of studies may have been perused during the course of the research, but only those that help substantiate the researcher's contention, idea, or concept are reviewed. Theoretical framework is, therefore, indispensable in any serious research, especially at the higher level.

The Research Procedure

It is necessary for the researcher to give a careful and detailed analysis of the procedures for the proposed research. He should outline the entire research plan, describing not only what he intends to do but how he intends to do it. He should state the data that will be used for its ultimate realization. It is not out of the way to succinctly speculate on the utility of the different categories of data or basic assumptions made earlier. Finally, he should state what devices will be employed in data collection and assess the reliability of these devices and the method of data analysis.

Time Schedule

Academic research projects like theses and dissertations usually require definite deadlines for the submission of the final product. Similarly, funded research, especially those derived from grants by organizations, sometimes involves time limitations and definite deadlines. This creates the need for appropriate budgeting of the time available to the researcher. The time schedule also helps the researcher to budget his time effectively and more systematically towards the completion of the research.

Six

REVIEW OF SCHOLARSHIP

The art of reading is a process of mutual seduction, whereby the reader and the read arouse each other's fantasies, expose each other's dreams. It is when we think we penetrate the text's disguises that we are usually most deluded and most ignorant, for what we see is nothing but our unknown selves.

- **Maud Ellman**

Reading is not a passive process by which we soak up words and information from the page, but an active process by which we predict, sample, and confirm or correct our hypotheses about the written text.

- **Constance Weaver**

Review of scholarship is a comprehensive analytical appraisal of all scholarly material available in the area of investigation. Referring to it merely as a review of literature may not clearly show the enormity of the degree of scholarship expected in this important part of the research process. This comprehensive analysis includes verbal reports, written documents including theses, dissertations, conference proceedings, and information stored in computer databases. It takes into consideration the significant areas of the subject of research, shows the significant scholars involved in intellectual discussions on the subject, and their special contributions to scholarship in the area of investigation. It identifies aspects of the research area that have generated controversy or debate by scholars and discusses the areas of the subject that have enjoyed a consensus of opinion among scholars. It should not be a mere annotation of a bibliography or a descriptive list of the scholarship available in the area of investigation. A good review of scholarship helps the researcher to identify a lacuna in the research area.

Whether it is theoretical or experimental, analytical or critical, an appropriate review of scholarship should summarize, evaluate, clarify and integrate all shades of scholarship in the area of investigation into an organized form; the relationship between the different scholarly sources must be identified, articulated and ranked in relation to its utility in the extant research. The main aim is to intimate the reader with the present state of scholarship in the area of investigation and assess their contribution to the advancement of knowledge in the area generally and on the topic particularly.

A good review of scholarship must, therefore, embody both summary and synthesis and should be relevant, appropriate and useful to the study being undertaken. It is a test of the researcher's ability to effectively familiarize himself with the available scholarship in the area of investigation, as well as his ability to apply critical and analytical principles in the research process. The works reviewed should be assessed in relation to their objectivity, provenance and persuasiveness.

Organizing the Review

It is necessary for the researcher to create an organizational method for the review to avoid the danger of making a random compilation of the scholarly sources identified. The following organization should be taken into consideration in crafting the review of scholarship:

1. Chronological Arrangement

This is the method of reviewing the scholarly sources according to their publication dates. It reveals the chronological progression of the study and assures the researcher of some degree of relative continuity in the review. One major advantage of this arrangement is that it helps the researcher to analyze how ideas develop from one another, showing how an argument is further explicated in more recent scholarship. It is important to organize the chronological review of scholarship in sub-sections, each sub-section dealing with the significant time or period of the review.

2. Thematic Arrangement

This kind of arrangement involves the organization of the review around topics or issues. The researcher should identify the major themes, topics or issues in the area of investigation and organize the review around them. In the thematic arrangement the researcher is advised to use time progression in the organization of the ideas, themes or issues identified. Each theme, topic or issue should be reviewed in chronological order, taking their publication dates into consideration. Sub-sections should be used to itemize the themes, topics or issues identified.

3. Methodological Arrangement

This approach focuses attention on the method used by the scholars whose works are being reviewed. It does not focus on the content, theme or chronology but essentially on method. This is recommended for the researcher whose area of investigation has been variously explicated through significant methodological approaches.

4. Categorical Arrangement

In a categorical arrangement, the researcher divides the sources identified into positive and negative categories. For instance, the review could be categorized into two reflecting the scholars who support a particular position and those who are opposed to it. This is very important especially if there are distinctive opposing issues competing for recognition in the research area.

Sources to be Reviewed

Scholarship in an area of investigation can be identified from the following areas:

Books

These are scholarly works published in the area of investigation. Care should be taken in determining appropriate books to be included in the review. Textbooks should be used with care since the information contained in them is usually mainly pedagogical and less oriented to research. However, they constitute a good starting point, especially for the beginning researcher. It should be remembered that books take a longer time to see print, and as a result, the information they contain may not be up-to-date right from its publication date.

Journal Articles

Journal articles are essays published in scholarly journals. Some journals are reputable and deal with special areas, while some merely cater for the interest of the general audience. Articles appearing in reputable journals are usually refereed, making them relevant and reliable. Journal articles are very useful in research because their contents are usually concise and current.

Conference Papers/Proceedings

Conference papers present current scholarly research in an area of investigation. If the paper is significant, it is usually published in the Conference proceedings. Conference papers present the latest data and are usually authored by practicing researchers in the field.

Government Reports

These are reports of research commissioned by government agencies or other corporate bodies. The findings provide useful scholarly information to researchers, especially if the studies were carried out by academic researchers.

Theses and Dissertations

These represent research projects submitted for the award of a degree. Some of them contain intensive research, but many are written merely to fulfill the requirements of the prescribed degree and may not have been properly researched. Such material should be used with care.

Interconnectivity Network (Internet)

This represents information stored electronically and meant to be sourced through the computer. Internet sources should be used with caution because anybody can post anything on the Internet. Furthermore, many Internet sources are directed to the general audience and are therefore not reliable or appropriate for serious scholarly research. However, there are many very good sources on the Internet and some of the sources are very useful. For instance, many journals are now pi electronically, and if they are refereed, they have the same Malus as a printed journal in terms of quality and reliability.

CD-ROMS

Most CD-ROMS are meant for the general audience and may not be reliable enough as research materials. Many CD-ROMS contain credible materials useful for research, cepcially if such materials are stored in academic libraries.

Magazines

Though many magazines are intended for the general audience, there are specialized magazines in many academic areas, which usually contain specialized articles or documented information that could be useful to the researcher. It is always advisable not to base a whole argument on magazines but to seek supplementary material to lend more intellectual strength to the magazine article.

Newspapers

Newspapers are intended for the general public and should not be used in the review of scholarship by a serious researcher. If the source is a feature article written by a specialist, such material should be used with caution or completely disregarded as a major scholarly source that deserves inclusion in the researcher's review of scholarship.

Writing a Good Review of Scholarship

The first point to be considered in writing a good review of scholarship is selection. Since the researcher does not need to review all the sources identified, the process of selection becomes very important. Only the most significant sources identified should be selected, and the researcher should ensure that each source chosen relates directly to the focus of the study.

Second, there is a need for cautious rendering of the material being reviewed. The writing should be done with care and caution and be in the nature of discursive prose. The sources should be summarized and synthesized. Quotations should be grossly limited, and the researcher is urged to use his own words completely when paraphrasing a source. The opinion of the scholar whose work is being reviewed should be accurately articulated.

Finally, there is a need for consistency in tone. Though the review presents the ideas and opinions of others, it is important for the researcher to create and maintain his own distinct voice throughout the review.

Seven

INVESTIGATIVE TECHNIQUES

The real voyage of discovery consists not in seeking new landscapes but in having new eyes.

- **Marcel Proust**

The sturdiest tree is not found in the shelter of the forest but high upon some rocky crag, where its daily battle with the elements shapes it into a thing of beauty.

- **Anon**

Documentary Research

Documentary research is a type of research dedicated to the learning of new facts through the study of documents or records. Though this kind of research is very popular with the humanities its use is extended to all academic areas. Because historians use it very regularly as a result of its usefulness in investigating the events of the past, many people erroneously perceive documentary research as a part of the historical method.

Documentary research is considered the oldest form of research. Aristotle extensively used this research method in his renowned work. Poetics. In this monumental work, Aristotle examined the existing documents of the period and came up with pertinent generalizations on the matter and manner of dramatic art and literature.

The aim of documentary research is to carefully examine documents and records for the purpose of forming conclusions that would establish new facts or appropriate generalizations about past events. From these generalizations, facts are ultimately established. Apart from records, documentary research can also be used in academic areas like Geology for the study of fossils to reveal more about the past than documents.

The major principle used in documentary research is the critical examination and evaluation of documents and records in order to reach pertinent conclusions. By making generalizations about past events we inevitably come to conclusions which may help us in understanding the present and ultimately predict the future.

Reasons for Undertaking Documentary Research

There are four reasons for undertaking documentary research:

(a) To understand the documents and assess how they came into being;

(b) To learn facts about their existence and being;

(c) Learn something about their authors or the people that originated them as well as the events that led to their origination;

(d) To draw hypotheses from them and, from these hypotheses come to conclusions that would assist us in interpreting them with intellectual honesty.

Sources of Materials for Documentary Research

A variety of source materials find utility in documentary research. They range from books and official records to newspaper and eyewitness accounts. Even personal letters and diaries of eminent personalities that helped in shaping the past are copiously examined as well as archaeological and geological deposits. Other important sources of documentary research include biographies, autobiographies, memoirs, historical studies and literary and philosophical writings. Because of their complexity, identifying and locating these sources is the first major task of the documentary researcher.

Critical Evaluation of Sources

Though identification and location are paramount, the actual task of the documentary researcher is critical evaluation. Here, two methods of examination and evaluation are necessary: external and internal.

External evaluation, generally referred to as external examination, is the process of determining the authenticity of the document so located. In the case of personal letters and official documents, for instance, their genuineness has to be established before their evaluation and eventual interpretation. Scholars make stringent efforts to test the genuineness and authenticity of the documents located for research purposes. These include checking the handwriting in manuscripts and comparing them with the confirmed handwriting of the author, checking the signature, and even subjecting the document to physical and chemical analysis. Determining the genuineness and authenticity of the document is so important in the documentary research process that new methods of determining authenticity have been developed for greater effectiveness. These include the use of ultraviolet rays and fluorescent photography.

Internal critical evaluation of a document is principally concerned with the content of the document. It logically and critically appraises the meaning of the document and assesses the accuracy of its contents. It is not enough to establish authenticity if the contents are not exactly accurate. For instance, if the words and symbols are not in tandem with the known forms used during the period, the accuracy of the document as research material will be in doubt.

The need to examine the individual words and phrases of the author Is important in order to discern the hidden meaning lying under them. This is very necessary in documents like books, biographies, autobiographies and memoirs.

Ideas and phrases used in the document should be painstakingly studied along with contemporaneous references. This is necessary because certain meanings and inferences could be attached to those statements at the time the document was originated. Sometimes this could lead the researcher to the evaluation of historical, linguistic, economic, philosophical, psychological and socio-political situations of the period when a particular document was written. This should be executed with caution in order to prevent the danger of reading unintended meanings into the document or to refute it because it slightly differs from the known philosophical thinking of its age.

Biographical Criticism Versus Deconstruction

It is necessary to discuss these terms briefly to show how they can easily infect documentary research in a positive or negative way.

Biographical Criticism

Documentary research fosters the extension of investigation to such areas as biography, histories of ideas, institutions and organizations. Influences and editing. Biographical research, particularly, implies that facts about a document can be truthfully discerned through an examination of the author's life, character and achievements since such facts are assumed to influence his thoughts and direct his pen.

Many literary scholars see the need to investigate the lives of authors; the researcher in education investigates the lives of educators and science researchers and the lives of other scientists. Unfortunately, these facts sometimes have little or no connection with the document itself, and the connections between the document and the biography and socio-political situations of the author become mainly speculative and, at times, obtrusive. This thinking was essential in the evolution of deconstruction as a critical concept.

Deconstruction

Deconstruction is a poststructuralist theory of critical thought which considers the idea of a unified document illusory because the meaning in a document is indeterminate. An extension of the concept of hermeneutics, this theory was given impetus by Jacques Derrida. To Derrida, a document is replete with a multiplicity of meanings because there is no fixed system of knowledge and, therefore, no definite, absolute meaning in a text. Meaning, Derrida maintains, is always "in a state of contention and flux." Knowledge organized or structured around a centre is ultimately structured around an absolute truth, a situation that could be applicable to a legal document or medical diagnosis, not critical interpretation. Examining the biography of the author as a basis for interpreting a document is an unnecessary exercise in applied intellectual gossip. As I have stated in *Visions and Re-Visions*,

The text [of a document] should be perceived as an entity within itself, and its interpretation should not be encumbered by unnecessary intrusive meanings. It is the text that speaks, and no prior or external presence ought to be considered in its analysis (8).

Derrida argues that since the author is no longer the source of meaning in a text, deconstruction becomes an accessory to the death of the author. The documentary researcher should, therefore, be careful and cautious in the use of external material from outside the document in the interpretation and evaluation of that text.

HISTORICAL RESEARCH

The word history comes from the Greek word "historia", which means "searching to find out". Robert Jones Shafer, in *A Guide to Historical Method,* defines history as "a discipline, a field of study that has developed a set of methods and concepts by which historians collect evidence of past events, evaluate that evidence, and present a meaningful discussion of the subject. "Historical research, therefore, deals with evidence. It involves the description of past events or facts written in the spirit of critical inquiry. It embraces the whole areas of the human past. The data must be viewed from a historical perspective as part of the process of social development rather than as isolated attitudes, events or facts.

Historical research abounds in all areas of scholarship and is a very comprehensive and scholarly activity. The researcher using the historical method should, therefore, avoid the temptation of erroneously thinking that the aim of historical research is merely to interpret the past. Historical research attempts to establish facts and arrive at conclusions concerning the past. The historian systematically and objectively locates, evaluates, and interprets evidence from which one can learn about the past. Based on the evidence gathered the historian draws conclusions regarding the past so as to increase our knowledge of how and why past events occurred and the process by which the past became the present. Historical research, therefore, does not aim at reconstructing and interpreting the past solely for the purpose of obtaining knowledge about the past but also serves as an engine which generates light on the present situation, as the case may be.

Clearly speaking, every piece of news becomes history even a minute after its first appearance. Therefore, historical research involves every human being. When one reflects on his life and re-reads a letter or looks into his diary he is involved in a kind of historical research.

In scholarly activities, historical research takes a more formalized shape. It is a systematic and scientific research which not only adopts a historical perspective in its methodology but also depends basically on historical evidence for materials. It investigates, experiments, evaluates, discovers, recalls, analyzes and reconstructs past trends, attitudes, achievements and facts in order to refresh the memory, proffers new dimensions to an issue, clarifies current problems, discover new knowledge or interpret existing ones in fresh perspective.

Basic Characteristics of Historical Research

The basic conception of the historical researcher is an interpretation of past events with the aid of appropriate points of reference. The major interpretative perspectives in historical research are the personal or biographical, the spiritual, the scientific, the economic, the geographical, and the sociological. A rewarding interpretation of history can be achieved by adopting any of these perspectives. Apart from these, historical research also involves eclectic interpretation, an approach that recognizes the fact that social events are interrelated.

Methodology in historical research follows the same pattern as other major research techniques: definition of a problem, formulation of a hypothesis, systematic collection of data and confirmation or disconfirmation of hypothesis. But unlike some other research methods, the researcher can neither manipulate nor control any of the variables. He is also incapable of the past events.

Collection of Data in Historical Research

Collection of data in historical research is multifarious and yields two broad types of data: documents and relics. Documents are written records, while relics are archaeological or geological remains. For written documents, local archives are indispensable. In developed countries, every County area has well-documented local archives where historical researchers can consult maps, wills, inventories, deeds, registers, diaries, letters, account books, minute books, pictures, handbills, and other relevant information that would be helpful in their research effort.

For oral information, historical research relies mainly on extensive and in-depth sampling in order to detect deliberate omissions or distortions of fact. This can be done by obtaining information from a large number of people in a particular research area. The technique of comparative knowledge is essential in this regard. By this means, the interpretation of data is executed in the light of the totality of the oral tradition of the community and compared with the oral traditions of related or neighboring communities in order to either establish authenticity or deflate exaggerations.

Interdisciplinary (or multidisciplinary) techniques are very essential in historical research in order to ensure independent interpretation of facts. For example, lexico statistics and glottochronology have been found to be useful in estimating the separation of time between two languages or two dialects of the same language. Invariably the radiocarbon method for dating archaeological material has been useful in obtaining accurate dates when artifacts were deposited in the distant past.

EXPERIMENTAL RESEARCH

From the early twentieth century, when the Swiss entomologist Felix Santschi carried out an experimental study of the behaviour of the common ant, experiment has remained an important technique in the research process.

The word experiment comes from the Latin word ex-periri, which means "to try out". Experimental research is an empirical approach to research which is used to investigate particular types of research questions for the solution of specific problems. It is the most effective method of solving practical problems for the supporting or negation of theoretical assumptions.

Experimental research designs are, therefore, concerned with the manipulation of one or more independent variables for the determination of their effect on dependent variables. These designs are used where there is both time priority and consistency in causal relationships and where the magnitude of the correlation is great. The main purpose of experimental design is the elimination of alternative hypotheses.

Categories of Experimental Research

Experimental research can be categorized into five distinct canonical procedures:

(a) the methods of agreement;
(b) the methods of difference;
(c) the joint method;
(d) the method of residues
(e) the method of concomitant variations.

Controlled experiment is a method of comparing the results yielded by an experimental sample against a control sample. Usually, the control sample shares the same identity with the experimental sample except for a single aspect. It is this situation that is tested in the control sample. This is very peculiar to laboratory experiments, where the achievement of experimental authenticity requires the replication of samples for the test being performed. It enables the researcher to obtain both positive and negative control. If a replicate sample is found to be clearly inconsistent with the results obtained from other samples, it can be considered an experimental error and eventually discarded. While a positive control is similar to the actual experimental test and sometimes the quadrant of a standard curve, the negative control produces a negative result.

Natural experiments, also referred to as quasi-experiments, rely entirely on the observation of the variables of the system under study instead of manipulating one or a few variables. Collection of data in natural experiments is carried out in such a way as to ensure that contributions are obtained from all variables.

Observational studies, as a part of experimental research, is a kind of experiment that lacks probabilistic equivalency between groups. The results obtained from observational studies are considered to be more prone to selection bias and, hence, less convincing than those obtained from designed experiments.

Field experiment, another kind of experimental research, does not involve the use of the laboratory but engage in observation in a natural setting.

Experimental research in animals is more abundant than those in man. This is because it is almost impossible for human beings to be studied in the laboratory, hence the need to study them experimentally outside the laboratory. To do this three experimental praxis are used: one group method, the parallel-group method, and the rotation-group method. It should be noted that the selection of animals or human subjects to be subjected to experimental study should be large enough to make the sample adequate and the conclusions authentic.

Though the experimental method is considered the most scientific of all the investigative techniques, it has many pitfalls. To ameliorate the possibility of possible errors, the following remedial measures are necessary:

1. Every experiment should not be conducted once. It should be repeated several times before a convincing result is recorded.
2. All the factors that might affect the results of the experiment should be identified with care and kept under constant control.
3. All the instruments and materials to be used in the experiment must be seen to be accurate and in good condition.

SURVEY RESEARCH METHOD

The survey is a non-experimental, descriptive research method of obtaining exact facts about a current situation through sampling a population. A population, by definition, is a set of objects or persons possessing at least one common characteristic.

Survey research is a very valuable method of obtaining data on a non-observable phenomenon in order to learn the status of something. This investigative technique is also described in various names like descriptive study, the normative survey or the status study. It is not restricted to fact-finding since its results can be used for the formulation of significant principles of knowledge as well as the solution of scholarly problems.

The first recorded major survey in world history dates back to the ancient Roman Empire when Augustus Caesar made a decree requiring every inhabitant of the empire to report to his city of birth for a census. Caesar's survey shows that most surveys involve counting and that the results of such surveys help in the formulation of theories and serve as tools for social and economic reform. Survey data are usually collected through the use of questionnaires or direct interviews and can be either qualitative or quantitative.

Public Opinion Surveys are one of the most popular methods in the survey process. It is often used to determine the opinion of the general public on a number of issues. For instance, the market survey can give the marketer the opinions of potential buyers and thus minimize the incidence of errors on the part of the manufacturer. Market surveys are also used to obtain concrete information on the status of a product by surveying people's reactions to it, the perceived effectiveness of the product, and possible areas of dislike.

Cross-sectional and Longitudinal Surveys

There are two basic types of surveys: cross-sectional surveys, used to gather information on a population at a single point in time, and longitudinal surveys, used to gather data over a period of time. Longitudinal survey, on the other hand, yields itself to three distinct types, namely, trend studies, cohort studies, and panel studies.

While trend studies focus on a particular population which is repeatedly sampled and scrutinized, cohort studies also focus on a particular population but samples and studies it more than once. Panel studies attempt to discern the reason for the occurrence of changes in the chosen population. Of the three methods of longitudinal studies, panel studies tend to be more expensive, involve more time and suffer from high attrition rates.

Sampling Procedures

A sample is a method of taking a portion of a population to represent the entire population. It is used on the assumption that a portion of a population can serve as an adequate and reliable representative of that universe and can adequately be used to make pertinent conclusions on the nature of that universe. A representative sample occurs when there is an accurate representation of the population being studied.

The process of sampling is to gather information from sources from a cross-section of a population used to represent the entire universe. Four major kinds of sampling will be discussed here: random sampling, stratified sampling, double sampling and cluster sampling.

Random Sampling

Random sampling is a method of drawing a sample at random without any form of bias or interest. The portion of a population is drawn in such a way as to give every member of that population an equal opportunity to be selected. For instance, the researcher can make a list of persons needed for the research and select every third person from the list until he gets the desired number that is deemed representative of the universe.

Invented by Sir Ronald Fisher, random sampling fosters the possibility of equal representation because it lacks individual predictability since no choice is predetermined by another.

The advantage of random sampling is that since there is no significant law guiding selection, it is unbiased and makes for greater accuracy.

Stratified Sampling

Stratification is a method of dividing a population into sub-groups, with each sub-group representing a significant paradigm. It is a process of dividing a sample into constituent parts. Its aim is to make the sample truly representative of the population. For instance, the researcher could divide the population of a town into stratified groups like young people, retired people, working people, poor people and wealthy people. Other factors like gender can also be used.

A researcher sampling dramatic literature can stratify them into genres: tragedy, comedy, melodrama, tragic-comedy, and farce. These genres can also be further stratified for better representation. Tragedy, for instance, can be further stratified into Classical, Elizabethan, Romantic and Modern, as the case may be.

Double Sampling

Double sampling is a method of drawing a second sample from the population, whether the drawn sample constitutes respondents or non-respondents. The aim is to check the reliability of the information received. The second sample becomes necessary if the researcher feels that there is a likelihood of the existence of a significant non-respondent population in the first sample.

Cluster Sampling

This method of sampling lists the population in clusters and selects respondents from representative units of the sample. Cluster sampling is prone to error because the clusters could contain the same information.

Steps in Designing a Sample

There are four steps to be taken into consideration in designing a sample of a research project. The first is the definition of the population. The second is the creation of a list of units in the population. The third is the determination of the size of the sample that would be representative of all the characteristics being studied. The fourth is drawing appropriate units from the list in such a way that the list represents the entire universe.

THE INTERVIEW METHOD

Personal interviews are one of the most effective means of obtaining pertinent information in survey research. This is because personal interview accords the researcher the rare opportunity of face-to-face interaction with the respondent. He can ask follow-up questions, direct the destination of the interview to significant issues, and seek clarification where necessary.

Steps in Conducting an Interview

The first step in conducting an interview is to make a definite appointment with the respondent. The researcher should ensure that enough time is allotted to the interview to afford him the opportunity to cover all the items listed for the interview.

After obtaining an appropriate appointment, the researcher should embark on adequate planning. He should make a detailed outline of the interview process, listing questions in their order of importance. Follow-up questions should be carefully designed from the main questions. The questions should be specific and carefully worded. If there is more than one respondent to be interviewed, the researcher should ensure that the questions are asked in exactly the same way.

When interviewing the respondent, the researcher should ensure that he is alone. The interview should be suspended if there is an intrusion. The aim is to ensure that the intruder does not divert the attention of the respondent or influence his answers in any way.

Every question should be clearly stated and its full import made clear to the respondent. If there is a need for further explanation or clarification, the researcher should not hesitate to do so. It is necessary for the respondent to understand the tly in order to obtain his/her correct opinion.

The researcher should be aware of the fact that sometimes a respondent could be reluctant to release confidential information. When such happens, he should offer an assurance to the respondent that the information being sought is purely for research purposes. He should explain the nature and purpose of the study to calm and reassure the respondent.

A good interviewer should desist from injecting his own ideas or bias into the phrasing of the question in order to obtain a specific answer. He should also refrain from asking embarrassing questions.

Throughout the session, the interviewer should try to win and maintain the trust of the respondent by demonstrating that he is honest and dependable.

Recording

Accurate recording is very crucial in interviews. The answers obtained should be recorded during the interview and not recalled from memory afterwards. It is more preferable for the researcher to use the actual words of the respondent in the research report. If he uses a tape recorder, he should ensure that the transcription is carefully and cautiously done so that the recorded answers should be definite and unequivocal and not prone to misinterpretation or misunderstanding.

THE QUESTIONNAIRE

Definition

A questionnaire is a series of written questions carefully formulated, whose answers are intended to aid the researcher in the solution of the research question. A well-written questionnaire is regarded as a substitute for the oral interview, though it lacks the advantage of face-to-face interaction with the Respondents.

The questionnaire is either mailed to respondents or administered by enumerators. If mailed to the respondents, each questionnaire should be accompanied by a letter stating the purpose of the research and gently requesting the respondents' assistance in completing the desired questions. He should also enclose a self-addressed stamped envelope to facilitate the return of the questionnaire.

Designing a Good Questionnaire

The first step in designing a good questionnaire is brevity. The questions should be as brief as possible in order to make for clarity and avoid the possibility of wasting the respondent's time.

Second, the information being sought must not be accessible to the researcher. If it is clear to the respondent that such information is accessible to the researcher, he will feel reluctant to supply it.

Third, the subject of inquiry must not be considered trivial by the respondent. It should have enough importance to justify the time and effort employed by the respondent in attending to the questionnaire.

Fourth, the questions should show clearly that the aim of the researcher is to obtain factual data. It should have no place for the representation of the respondent's opinions or impressions.

Fifth, the items should be carefully arranged, and the wording of every question should be clear to the respondent. If the question is clear and comprehensible to the respondent, the researcher will be sure to obtain appropriate answers to the questions.

To ensure clarity, words with double meaning should be clearly defined or even avoided. It is more preferable to use simple, clear, comprehensible terms in the design of a good questionnaire. The researcher should be aware that imperfections in the design of the questionnaire will ultimately result in inaccuracies in the answers obtained from the respondents.

The researcher should make cogent efforts to ensure the return of the completed questionnaire. If some respondents fail to return the questionnaire in time, a follow-up letter should be written to such respondents, gently soliciting the return of the questionnaires.

Validation of the Questionnaire

In order for the researcher to ensure that the designed questionnaire is satisfactory, it should be subjected to an appropriate validation process. The aim is to ensure that the questionnaire will effectively yield accurate and reliable data.

The best way to validate a questionnaire is to test it by inflicting the questions on some of the persons who have been chosen to receive it. This should be done in the form of personal interviews with the chosen respondents. This test is bound to reveal the faults contained in the questionnaire. It will also reveal the propensity of the questionnaire to yield reliable data.

In the final analysis, the researcher should remember that it is the critical analysis of the data collected through the questionnaire and the logical conclusions reached that reflect the excellence of the research report.

OBSERVATIONAL RESEARCH

Definition

Observational research technique is à method of searching for facts by making observations within natural settings. This kind of research presents and analyzes data that results from the personal observation of the researcher. Observational research, therefore, focuses on data personally collected through observation. It presents a valid and comprehensive description of social behaviour because the behavioral norms of the population have been personally observed by the investigator. It does not employ different kinds of measurement but focuses on the examination of what happens, how it happens and what it means to the participants, all seen through the acute and diligent observatory eyes of the investigator.

In an observational study, the researcher does not only observe. He also records the happenings without any form of interaction with the participants. He stays like the invisible member of the audience and should be careful not to attract the attention of the subjects being observed. To achieve this, he could stay in a hidden but clear point observing the proceeding without interruption. Alternatively, he could mix with the audience and get as close as possible to the performers, but making sure that he is not identified as a researcher. His major goal is to see and record the actual behaviour of the subjects without disclosing his identity.

Observational research is considered to have very strong validity because the researcher carefully observes the subjects and collects concrete information on their actual behaviour. Findings in observational research reflect the attitude of a particular population in a particular setting and are, therefore, not prone to generalization.

Necessity for Observational Research

Observational research is necessary in a situation where the researcher feels that he may not obtain accurate answers from respondents due to bias, prejudice, or secrecy. A theatre student studying the masquerade performance of a given society, for instance, may not obtain accurate answers and pertinent information from respondents because some aspects of the performance are clothed in secrecy. Such sensitive social issues are better reduced to observational research or, more appropriately, participant observation. Though the observational researcher may not observe attitudes, he can observe behaviour and, from the observation, make inferences about attitudes.

Ethical Considerations in Observational Research

Because observational research requires observation and sometimes interaction with the group, some ethical considerations should be taken into account before, during, and after the research has been conducted. Some of them are:

Informed Consent The researcher should consider Whether or not the participants need to have full knowledge of what is involved in the research being undertaken.

Involvement of Harm and Risk - The investigator should ensure that there is no possibility of the investigation hurting or constituting a risk to the participants.

Existence of Honesty and Trust - The researcher should be honest and truthful in presenting the data collected.

Intrusion of Privacy- Every observational study involves Intrusion of privacy. The researcher should ensure that the study will not intrude too deeply into the behaviour of the group. If such a possibility exists, he should design a method of maintaining the anonymity of the group.

Intervention and Advocacy - The researcher should realize that there is the danger of the group being hostile or harmful. He should, therefore, make adequate provisions to avert the possibility of this occurrence.

Observational Variables

Observations can be descriptive, inferential or evaluative. While descriptive observation requires the investigator to observe and record the proceeding without making inferences, inferential observation requires him to make inferences about the observation. Evaluative observation, on the other hand, requires the researcher to make both an inference and a judgment from the observed behaviour.

Types of Observations

There are two major types of observation: direct and unobtrusive observation. In direct observation, the researcher does not hide the fact that he is watching the proceeding. The subjects know he is there and is probably recording their actions. The danger of direct observation is that the presence of the researcher may influence the behaviour of the subjects and deter them from displaying their true behaviour. This can be overcome by long-term observational studies.

In *unobtrusive observation*, the individuals are unaware of the presence of the investigator. Therefore, there is no fear that the presence of an observer may influence the behaviour of members of the group. Many scholars consider unobtrusive observation an invasion of privacy and, therefore, discourage it. Other scholars, however, consider it a more reliable method of data collection because of their belief that a more reliable data could emerge if the researcher is a disguised field analyst.

Major Differences

One major difference between the two methods is the manner of recording the information being observed. The direct observer may take down notes in the full view of the population or even employ the use of electronic devices. Because he is disguising his identity, the unobtrusive researcher may not have such an advantage.

Critical and Pre-critical Response to Observation

The process of observation can take the form of pure pleasure or subjected to scholarly study. When one approaches 2025/0385 without the necessary scholarly tools for measurement, he merely experiences a precritical response to the proceeding being observed. Here it is necessary to give a long quotation from my previous work on the subject.

A group of university students decide to spend their free period watching a masquerade performance. They head for the village square where the performance is taking place. The mingling of other peers as they discuss excitedly about the performance and its interesting aspects increases their pleasure. They perceive the aesthetics of the costume, make-up, diversity of movement, and the coordination of dramatic action and their suggestive archetypal messages. What they perceive is a precritical response to the performance.

From another angle, another group of students emerges, this timeless boisterous and excited. They are students of Theatre Arts, accompanied by their lecturer, who is leading them on field research. Through observation, they are expected to analyze the performance. They are versed in the theories of performance and the exigencies of dramatic productions. On the general level, they receive the same experience as the first group, but their special intellectual knowledge places them on another pedestal since they are now able to use their special knowledge to comprehend and analyze the performance. This knowledge neither obfuscates their pleasure nor nullifies their precritical response to the performance. Rather, it intensifies or complements it. The knowledge merges with the feeling to produce a kind of ego-involvement, which leads to the application of learned interpretative techniques to the intellectual analysis of the proceeding. This is the critical response (*Visions* 3).

PARTICIPANT OBSERVATION

Meaning

Participant observation is a research technique where the researcher joins the group being studied in order to take part in their activities. During the participation he records and describes his experiences, observations, impressions and interpretations. He should document the happenings in a comprehensive manner and try to remain as unbiased as possible.

The main assumption of participant observation is that the researcher is presumed to gain a deeper and more valid understanding of the subject being studied than can be obtained from the questionnaire, interview and mere observation.

By participating in the happening, the researcher obtains latent information not only on what happens and how it happens but on why it happens. Participation is, therefore, considered an opportunity for in-depth, valid, comprehensive and systematic investigation into the activities of a particular group.

History and Development of Participant Observation

Participant observation, as a research tool, is rooted in anthropological studies, but it is now a valid research tool in almost all areas of study, including Theatre and Dramatic Arts, where it is found to be indispensable in studying the matter and manner of traditional theatre. It is necessary to state, however, that Humanities researchers spend less time in participant observation than sociologists. In sociological research, participant observation is quite close to ethnography, the difference being that the participant observer spends less time in the field than the ethnographer.

Participant observation gained impetus in the work of Abu RayhanBiruni (973-1048), a Persian anthropologist who is as the progenitor of this research technique. Birunicarried out personal research on the customs and religions of India. During this study, he engaged in participant observation by staying with the group, learning their language and studying their texts, and finally presenting his findings through the use of cross-cultural comparisons.

During the later part of the nineteenth century, this method was extensively used by Frank Hamilton Cushing in his comprehensive study of Zuni Indians. Participant observation as a research method became very popular and was seen to be a veritable tool in the study of non-Western societies during the second half of the twentieth century. With constant and improved use, participant observation was made more receptive to replicability and formal hypothesis testing. Such scholars as Bronislaw Malinowski and Edward Evans-Pritchard contributed extensively to the development of this research technique.

Difference between Observation and Participant Observation

The main difference between observation and participant observation is that in observation, the researcher is an outsider simply observing and documenting the event or behaviour under study. In participant observation, the researcher becomes a participant, taking part in the activity and, at the same time, documenting his observations in a careful and copious manner. He learns as an insider while remaining essentially an outsider, a researcher, and an investigator.

Difficulties in Participant Observation

One of the main difficulties in participant observation is that the participant observer may need to learn the language or dialect of the area being observed. In fact he needs to engage in a comprehensive study of the aphorisms and exigencies of the group before his participation. If this is done appropriately the researcher will succeed in establishing his legitimacy to the group.

The second problem is that participant observation is time-consuming because it requires the researcher to spend a considerable amount of time with the group. If this is not carefully executed, he runs the risk of violating the timetable for the submission of the research report.

Three, the participant observer may encounter difficulty in recording data. This is because it is difficult to engage simultaneously in recording and documentation while engaged in the act of participation and observation.

Four, the researcher may inadvertently sacrifice objectivity on the altar of subjectivity while writing the research report. Since research is inherently an exercise in objectivity, the researcher is supposed to show objectivity in his report by differentiating between description and interpretation. He should accurately report or describe what he sees and does so that an objective interpretation would inevitably emerge.

Advantages of Participant Observation

One major advantage of participant observation is that it affords the researcher the opportunity to engage in informal conversations and copious interactions with members of the population being studied. This will give him more reliable insight into difficult interpretations.

Furthermore, since it is an integral part of the iterative research process, data collected through participant observation can be used in the improvement of other research designs.

CONTENT ANALYSIS

Definition

Content analysis is a research tool that focuses on the actual content and internal features of media. Bernard Berelson gave a more appropriate definition of this important investigative technique when he stated that Content Analysis is "a research technique for the objective, systematic, and quantitative description of the manifest content of communications" (74). Apart from outlining the use of content analysis as a research tool, Berelson was one of the first scholars to engage in a critical analysis of current literature on the subject.

Content analysis is an objective way of determining and quantifying the existence of certain themes, concepts, characters, sentences, phrases and words within a text. Books, essays, newspaper articles and headlines, historical documents, speeches, advertising, dramatic texts, and, in fact, all aspects of communicative language can be studied through content analysis.

Coding

Coding is an important aspect of content analysis. The researcher using this investigative tool as a base for the study of any form of communicative language starts by coding the text or breaking it down into appropriate levels after which he examines them using either conceptual or relational analysis.

Conceptual Analysis

This is one of the two general categories of content analysis. Conceptual analysis is the establishment of the existence and frequency of significant concepts in a text. The researcher employing conceptual analysis as a research tool starts with a concept for study and goes on to examine and analyze the occurrences of that concept within the text. He then identifies research questions and codes the text into content categories in order to ensure the existence of an exhaustive and comprehensive treatment. He also ensures that the content categories are manageable enough to yield valid data. Using the process of selective reduction, the researcher then proceeds to analyze and interpret the characteristics of the message.

The main purpose of conceptual analysis is not merely to analyze the relationship between words but to quantify them and analyze the chosen concept using his research question as a focal point.

Relational Analysis

Relational analysis is a follow-up to conceptual analysis. Relational analysis mainly uses conceptual analysis to examine the relationships among the concepts appearing in a communicative document.

To ensure the utilization of a good relational analysis, the researcher should start by choosing the concepts that will be explored and analyzed. He should be careful not to choose too many categories in order to avoid the possibility of obscuring the eventual result. Invariably, inadequate or very few categories should also be avoided because of their tendency to yield invalid or unreliable conclusions.

Uses of Content Analysis

The main uses of content analysis are:

(a) To reveal international difference in the content of a text, article or any other form of communicative language; 05:13.2
(b) To identify the intentions, focus or trends of communication peculiar to individuals or groups;
(c) To identify, record, and describe attitudinal and behavioral responses to a system of communication,
(d) To determine the degree and existence of propaganda in a text as well as the psychological or emotional states of the subjects being investigated.

Advantages of Content Analysis in the Research Process

There are four main advantages of content analysis as an investigative technique:

1. By examining and analyzing texts, the researcher using content analysis can easily discern the central aspect of social interaction, which is a very important aspect of content analysis.
2. Because it is amenable to both quantitative and qualitative aspects of research, content analysis can be used to obtain concrete and valid information on historical and cultural issues.

3. Content analysis leads to a pungent statistical analysis of the coded form of the document being studied.
4. It is an unobtrusive means of analyzing and interpreting documents and human interaction.

Main Disadvantages

The main disadvantages of content analysis are both theoretical and procedural. First, like the participant observation, content analysis consumes a lot of time. The researcher should, therefore, be careful not to allow this investigative technique to violate his time frame.

Since context is important in the production of a text, content analysis has the propensity to disregard the context that produced the text being investigated.

Three, when relational analysis is employed in obtaining a higher level of interpretation in content analysis, the possibility of the existence of error becomes very high indeed.

Finally, because it apparently lacks a theoretical basis, content analysis may lead the inexperienced researcher to deal extensively with inferences rather than facts, especially when confronted with complex documents or texts.

BIBLIOMETRICS RESEARCH

Definition

Bibliometrics is an investigative technique that uses quantitative analysis and statistical data to describe patterns of publications within a particular academic area. It is a valid method of evaluating the influence of an author and can be used in a comparative fashion to analyze the relationship between two or more writers or a combination of works from one or different geographical areas. This investigative technique is particularly common in library and information science.

Areas of Bibliometrics Research

One important area of Bibliometrics research is citation analysis. This is used to establish relationships between major authors and their works. It uses citations in scholarly works to establish the following:

(a) Links between authors

(b) Links between fields

(c) Links between journals

(d) Links between scholarly works or between countries.

Citation analysis has been an effective way of determining the impact of an author on his academic area or even the entire scholarly region. This is done by counting the number of times the author has been cited by other scholars in the field. Unfortunately, this does not disclose whether the author is being cited in a positive or negative context,

Another area of Bibliometrics research is co-citation **coupling**. This is a method used to establish subject similarity between two documents. The relationship between two papers can be established by tracing how m many times both documents are cited simultaneously in one paper. The conclusion derived from this exercise is that the more the number of papers citing two articles together, the greater the conclusion that both have a significant relationship with one another.

Bibliographic coupling, another area of Bibliometrics research, operates by linking two papers that cite the same article. The theory guiding this activity is that if two papers cite the same article, then both papers can be said to have some significant scholarly relationship whether or not they cite each other.

Laws of Bibliometrics Research

The three laws of Bibliometrics research are Lotka's law of scientific productivity, Bradford's law of scatter, and Zipf's law of word occurrence.

Lotka's law of scientific productivity mainly describes the frequency of publication by authors in a given academic area. *Bradford's Law* of scatter, on the other hand, is generally concerned with giving general guidelines to librarians to enable them to discern the number of core journals existing in a particular academic area. *Zipf's law* of word occurrence is used to predict the frequency of words within a text.

EXPLORATORY RESEARCH

Meaning

When a researcher engages in an investigation, he is supposed to have a clearly defined problem to explore. When such a problem is inexistent or has not been clearly defined, the researcher resorts to exploratory research.

Exploratory research is conducted when there is no clearly defined problem to move the investigation to its logical conclusion. The aim of exploratory research is to determine the best research design, method of data collection, and selection of appropriate subjects for the extant research. When it is properly conducted, the main problems surrounding the research will become transparent.

Sources of Exploratory Research

The main source of exploratory research is secondary data. The first of such secondary data is a review of available scholarship in the research area. This helps the researcher to see what others have done, conclusions reached, arguments properly concluded, and those still begging for further exploration. In the process of this exploration he is bound to discover appropriate lacuna in the area of investigation.

Another available tool to the exploratory researcher is the use of qualitative research methods. He uses formal and informal interviews, case studies or pilot studies. Case studies, as a research tool, are forms of qualitative descriptive research used to study individuals or groups. Pilot studies, also called feasibility studies, are mini versions of a full-scale study.

The researcher may also resort to Internet research to explore interactive research methods. The most prominent internet sources in this area are Google and RSS. Through Google, comprehensive research results are traced. RSS is a viable source of up-to-date information on the Internet.

Purpose of Exploratory Research

The purpose of exploratory research is not technically to solve a problem but to provide valuable insight into an identified phenomenon. Because it's main objective is the gathering of preliminary information to assist the researcher in the definition of a problem and the development of hypotheses, exploratory research cannot be generalized.

DIALECTICAL RESEARCH

Meaning

Dialectical research, also referred to as dialectical enquiry or dialectical investigation, is a kind of qualitative research which uses the concept of dialectics as an investigative tool. Its aim is to discover truth through the examination and interrogation of competing ideas, perspectives or arguments.

Method

Dialectical research is exploratory in method. This is because it is devoid of any form of hypothesis testing. If there is any hypothesis to be tested, it is minimal and does not constitute the core of the research. The focus of dialectical research is the development of new or innovative understanding.

Method

Dialectical research is the direct opposite of empirical research. While empirical research is mainly concerned with the analysis and interpretation of data, dialectical research is concerned with ideas and arguments developed through appropriate logic. Though not a common research method, dialectical research can be applied to different kinds of problems in a variety of academic disciplines.

Eight

WRITING THE RESEARCH REPORT

The writing process is not linear, moving smoothly in one direction from start to finish. It is messy, recursive, convoluted, and uneven. Writers write, plan, revise, anticipate, and review throughout the process.

- **Maxine Hairston**

...reading must always aim at a certain relationship, unperceived by the writer, between what he commands and what he does not command of the patterns of the language he uses.

- **Jacques Derrida**

Research reports differ significantly in scope and treatment according to the academic discipline of the researcher. However, writing the report follows a conventional method in both style and form within all academic disciplines. All academic disciplines demand that the report be written with clarity, proper organization, appropriate presentation of material, and effective communication of ideas.

Whether the report is a thesis, dissertation, or even a term paper, it ought to follow a standardized pattern of organization.

Sections of the Report

The **preliminary section** of the report presents the following topics:

1. *The Title Page* – This includes the title of the topic, the name of the author, what the report is for (degree requirement, etc.), the name of the institution where the report is submitted, and the date of presentation.

2. *Dedication* (if any)

3. **The Acknowledgement** - This contains the acknowledgement of people who gave significant assistance to the researcher during the conduct of the investigation. Acknowledgements should be simple, honest, and devoid of flattery.

4. *Table of Contents* - In preparing the table of contents, the researcher should indicate the relationship between major and minor divisions in the table. This serves as an appropriate guide to the reader.

5. *List of Tables/Figures* (if any)

The **main body** of the report presents the following:

1. *The Introduction* - Ideally, the introduction should contain the following: statement of the problem, significance of the problem, purposes of the study, assumptions and limitations (if necessary), and definition of terms and concepts (if any). A good introduction should arouse the reader's interest.
2. *Appropriate Review of Scholarship* – Usually, this includes related and relevant literature in the research area, as well as analysis of previous research undertaken in the area of investigation.
3. *Research Design* – This includes procedures used in the study, sources of data, method of data collection, and strategies for data analysis.
4. *Presentation and Analysis* - This is usually done in chapters, according to the design of the study.

The Conclusion

In the conclusion, the researcher may use either the climatic or anti-climatic method. It is important to ensure that the conclusion concludes the report and does not open new arguments or pave the way for further discussion on the area of investigation.

In some academic areas, the researcher is expected to give the summary and conclusions to the study. In that case, the following information may be indispensable in marshalling the summary and conclusions to a research report: restatement of the problem, description of procedures used in the course of the research, significant findings and conclusions, and recommendations for further research. And

The researcher should remember that a good conclusion is designed to assist the reader in understanding the major points of his argument and establish their significance.

The Reference Section

Every research report ends with a reference section which indicates the sources used in the research. As will be apparent in the next chapter, references are arranged in alphabetical order, with the surname of the author listed first. Each entry is flushed with the left margin of the page, with subsequent lines indented five spaces.

If the report has an appendix, this should come immediately after the reference list. The pages of the appendix are numbered serially with the use of Arabic numerals. The appendix may include the following: tables and data used, printed forms of questionnaires used, or any letters obtained from the people interviewed.

Writing the First Draft

Writing the first draft of the research report gives the researcher a sense of joy and relief. The joy of putting ideas down on paper should be done freely without allowing it to be encumbered by worries about spelling, punctuation, and grammar. While writing the first draft, the researcher should be mainly concerned with ideas. In fact, the main purpose of the first draft is to give the researcher something to work on as well as something to work against. The draft should be done chapter by chapter in a progressive order.

Starting is the first main difficulty encountered by a neophyte. To make it easier, the researcher should use the outline very effectively. If it has been appropriately constructed, the problem will be minimal. The recommended method is to take a look at the listings on the outline, then write out the main points to be developed and follow up with supporting information that will help in the development of these points. The overall plan should be kept in mind in order to ensure uniformity.

If the researcher feels stuck in a particular part of the report, he should not allow that to derail him. He should move immediately to another topic on the outline, preferably in the same chapter, and start developing it. Stopping at that point will be a disadvantage. He should remember that the more one writes, the more efficiently he thinks. Writing is a form of logical thinking, understanding and discovery.

Another problem usually encountered by the beginning researcher is having too much information to utilize in the first draft. Sometimes, the researcher is led in the direction he never intended. That should not be conceived as a problem. When this happens, he should not hesitate to continue the exploration because what he considers a drifting may hold the key to a significant discovery as the report progresses. Revision period this new material could be integrated into the main study. During the revision period, new material could be integrated into the main study.

Development of Paragraphs

Writing is done in sentences and paragraphs. A good sentence and paragraph should be clear and developed in such a way as to bring the information to life. The researcher should not worry about the length of paragraphs at this point. During the revision period, they can be lengthened, shortened or merged.

Paragraphs can be developed with either details or examples. Details give a description of something, someone, or a place, while examples are illustrations of an idea, and they contain pertinent information to further elucidate the point being made.

The Rhetorical Method

During the first draft, the researcher should use rhetorical methods to develop paragraphs. Rhetorical method can be described as mental operations that assist in thinking through rhetorical problems. Major rhetorical methods of development include definition, description or narration, classification and division, cause-and-consequence analysis, and development of appropriate arguments.

Explanation shows the reader how something happened, while cause-and-consequence analysis helps in the establishment of why something happened, as well as the prediction of results. Comparison and contrast help in establishing similarities or differences, while classification and division help to establish order in the research report. Definition is an indispensable tool for the clarification of concepts and terms.

Comparison and contrast are methods that help the reader to appreciate a good research report. Comparison means pointing out similarities, while contrast means identifying differences. Two kinds of comparisons are important in the research report: metaphor and analogy.

A metaphor is a figure of speech that makes an indirect comparison to something, while an analogy directly compares the similarities between two things. The researcher should. However, be careful not to indulge in false analogy. In false analogy, there is an assumption that because two things are alike in some significant ways, they ought to be alike in everything.

Writing Time

It will be necessary to write as much as possible in one sitting.

This will help the researcher maintain trends of thought. Each major section should be written without interruption in order to ensure that the train of thought and consistency of style are maintained. Enough space should be left for corrections and insertions.

The researcher should be as logical as possible. Sub-divisions should be made to constitute a logical part of the topic under which it appears. Each item should be made as specific as possible and should deal with one concept.

Style

The style of the report should be objective, impersonal, and formal. The report should be in the third person, though some research areas allow researchers to use the first person. It is necessary to avoid contractions, slang, emotionalism, and extravagant language.

Organization

Each section of the report should contain the main idea, using appropriate transitional sentences or paragraphs. Each chapter requires a concluding paragraph leading to a transition. Irrelevancies, repetitions, and redundancy should be avoided.

Presenting Arguments

An argument is a group of at least two statements one of which constitutes the conclusion and the other the premises offered as support to a conclusion. Arguments present facts and a set of reasoning about facts that lead to certain opinions and conclusions. In a research report, the conclusion could be stated first, followed by a premise. Alternatively, one or more premises could be stated before the conclusion.

An argument can be stated in the form of an induction, comparison or causal analysis. In induction, the conclusion must arise from the data collected. The set of data must be presented before the conclusion is stated.

Deduction is the method of applying a generally accepted idea to data, after which conclusions are drawn based on the data. Deductions are sometimes presented in the form of syllogism. When this is done, the researcher should be careful not to misapply the syllogism or, make generalizations from insufficient information, or build assumptions into questions.

Comparison has been fairly discussed in this chapter, but it is necessary to add more information because of its importance in writing the research report. Simply stated, comparison is a method of comparing things to see their similarities and differences. In comparison we look for correlation and bring the things compared with the standards or other factors by which they are compared.

Causal analysis is the art of establishing causal relationships through inductive and deductive reasoning. In doing this, the researcher should be careful not to confuse fact with inference.

Writing Good Arguments

Arguments are written in the same process as other forms of writing. It goes through the process of planning, drafting, and revising. The first thing to bear in mind in marshalling an argument is to determine the purpose of the argument. The researcher should ensure that he understands what is at stake and the destination of the argument.

Second, the researcher should consider the different viewpoints and then take an arguable position on the topic after identifying and considering the issues that aggravate different opinions. This is because behind every effective argument lies a question that can generate more than one reasonable answer.

The third point is to distinguish between fact and opinion. Facts are reliable pieces of information verifiable through independent procedures, while opinions are assertions that may or may not be based on facts. To distinguish between fact and opinion, it is necessary to determine whether the statement can be proved and whether the proof is consistent. If it can be consistently proved to be true, it is a fact. If it can be disputed, it is an opinion. Effective arguments establish, in clear, unequivocal terms, the thinking that led to the claim.

Rhetorical Appeals that Shape Arguments

The Greek philosopher Aristotle was the first scholar to introduce three rhetorical appeals to a formal argument. These appeals are ethos, logos and pathos. Ethos means ethical appeal and deals with the establishment of the writer's credibility and trustworthiness. Since ethos alone cannot complete an argument, there is a need to apply the rhetorical concept of logos, which means logical appeal. The advantage of logos is that it demonstrates an effective use of reason and judicious use of appropriate evidence. Evidence utilized can be in the nature of facts, comparisons, expert opinions, observations, personal experiences, and statistics.

The rhetorical concept of pathos means the application of emotional appeal in an argument. This involves the use of language capable of stirring the feelings of the reader. The Researcher should use pathos mainly to establish empathy and authentic understanding, not to unduly influence or manipulate the reader.

Things to Avoid in Stating an Argument

To marshal a good argument, the researcher should avoid the following:

1. *Non sequitur* – This is a Latin phrase meaning "does not follow". Non sequitur means that the argument does not follow a logical order. It states that because the first part of a statement is true does not necessarily mean that the second part has to be true.
2. *Ad hominem* – This is an unnecessary personal attack on an opponent whose argument is being refuted. Such attacks are perceived as merely drawing the reader's attention away from the main issue being discussed.
3. *Appeals to Tradition* – This is a form of argument which recommends that something should be done in a particular way because that has been the tradition. The assumption here is that because something has been done in a particular way in the past, it should continue to be done in the same way.
4. *Bandwagon Effect* - This is a form of argument that follows a general opinion. It states that because everyone feels or thinks in a particular way, everyone else should follow the same method of thinking.

5. *Equivocation* - This is an argument that is merely in the nature of an assertion that falsely relies on the use of a term or statement in two different ways.
6. *False Analogy* – This is the assumption that because two things are alike in some ways, they must be alike in others.
7. *False Authority* – This form of argument assumes that an expert in one field can equally be considered credible in another field whether or not such fields are related.
8. *Guilt by Association* – This is an attempt to make others responsible for the beliefs or actions of another person. For instance, that a person attended the same school and belonged to the same profession or, religion or tribe does not mean that such people will all behave in the same manner.
9. *Hasty Generalization* – This kind of argument bases its conclusion on too little, exceptional, or biased evidence. To argue that a poor student remains consistently poor is a generalization. A poor student may improve in future.
10. *Oversimplification* - This is a kind of argument that leaves out relevant considerations for the purpose of implying that there is a single cause of or solution to a complex problem. Teaching people about abstinence does not necessarily wipe out unwanted pregnancies.
11. *Red Herring* - This form of argument is also called ignoring the question. It is a means of dodging the real issue in an argument by drawing attention to an irrelevant one.

Scientific Writing (The Laboratory Report)

In scientific writing clear and accurate presentation of facts is mandatory. Each fact is followed with a specific source, namely: the researcher's own experiments, studies conducted and published by other scholars, and surveys. Hence, the focus of the study should be on the data collected. Objectivity is also essential, though many contemporary scholars argue that no report can be completely objective.

The format of writing a laboratory report strictly follows the methods of scientific writing. It starts with a problem and a hypothesis and concludes with statements of proof, modification, or disapproval of the hypothesis. The following is an example of the format of a laboratory report that reflects the scientific method:

1. *The Abstract*- This states the problem and then goes on to summarize the results. The inclusion of an abstract is not compulsory. Some lecturers may not require their students to provide an abstract for a laboratory report.

2. *The Introduction* - The aim of this is to state the research question or hypothesis clearly and concisely. It also explains the scientific basis for the study, provides succinct background information on the subject of investigation and states the techniques to be used. In some cases, it may contain some citation references to relevant sources.
3. *The Methods and Materials* – This section should be in the form of a narrative describing the stages utilized in conducting the experiment. It should also enumerate the materials that were used, identify where the experiment was conducted, and describe, in a fairly comprehensive manner, the procedures followed. This section helps future researchers in the replication of the experiment.
4. *The Results* – This section should contain the report of the research results. It is done by describing major findings in the area of investigation. Such findings should be supported with properly labeled tables or graphs that show the empirical data.
5. *The Discussion* - This section should deal with the analysis of the results. It should show how the results are related to the goals of the study and make appropriate comments on the significance of the results. It is in this section that problems encountered in the course of the study are reported, and suggestions for further testing of the results are made.
6. *The References* - This section should embody the list of references used in the report. The list must be confined to the works that were referred to in the report. A comprehensive reference list is an indication of how widely the researcher has read and, ultimately, how viable the study is likely to be.

Revision Techniques

Revision is the act of taking another look at one's writing in order to identify and correct errors. Ineffective revision, the researcher assumes the status of the reader. By taking such a position, the researcher is able to evaluate how clearly the subject has been comprehensively covered in the report.

Sometimes, it is appropriate to edit and proofread during revision. The difference between revision and both editing and proofreading is that revision involves a thorough re-examination of the entire report in all its ramifications.

The main focus of editing is structural polish. It helps the researcher to reduce redundancy and choose words appropriately in order to achieve a more effective structuring of sentences. Proofreading, on the other hand, focuses mainly on the elimination of errors in writing, especially those of grammar and punctuation.

It is necessary to allow a passage of time between the draft and the revision. That is why it is important to finish your draft well ahead of time instead of struggling to edit the material immediately after writing. Allowing a few days is not bad. When the researcher eventually begins to revise after the time period, he will be more objective and critical.

The activities of revision, editing and proofreading can be done simultaneously. However, a careful researcher would engage in these activities differently. In that case, he reads the manuscript three times, revising, editing and proofreading, before it is finally handed in for typing.

Steps to Effective Revision

The art of revision is a creative activity and demands a large amount of creativity to ensure its effectiveness. Nevertheless, it is necessary to point out to the researcher the major areas of revision in order to ensure clarity and effectiveness in research writing. The researcher should remember that the difference between an excellent paper and an above-average paper may be in the effectiveness and ineffectiveness of revision.

Re-examination of the Content

The first step to effective revision is to re-examine the entire content of the paper. Orderly arrangements should be taken into consideration. Here, the outline becomes very useful because it is necessary to follow it appropriately, as the reader will rely on it for the progression of the report. The outline will help you ensure that the sections of the report are in their proper location.

Re-evaluation of Ideas

Re-evaluation of ideas is important in order to maintain appropriate focus. During this process, the researcher checks for sufficiency of information, the existence of extraneous material, redundancy, clarity, and conciseness of the ideas stated. The researcher can identify extraneous material by identifying and eliminating any information whose inclusion or exclusion hardly affects the development of the paper. If an idea is repeated in a different part of the study, the researcher should state this fact and, if necessary, state the need for repetition.

Check on Language

This is a very important part of revision. Check the quality of your grammar and ensure that there are absolutely no grammatical errors. Ensure that the sentences have both subject and predicate, that the punctuations are appropriate, and that the spelling of each word is correct and consistent. If a word is spelt in two different ways, follow the one that is most appropriate and be consistent with it.

There are many things to eliminate as the revision progresses, such as slang, bombastic words, jargon and colloquialisms. It is also necessary to eliminate abbreviations, acronyms and other such things that are not allowed in formal Standard English usage.

Punctuation also involves the correct use of colons, semicolons, hyphens, dashes, apostrophes, quotation marks, parentheses, brackets, and capitalized accordingly. And ellipses. Ensure that words are capitalized accordingly.

Tone

The researcher should remember that the tone of the report is a way of evaluating his use of the English language and a reflection of his attitude towards the subject of investigation. First-person and second-person pronouns, as well as contractions, should be clearly identified in the report and carefully eliminated as appropriate. Ultimately, the tone of the work should reflect self-confidence, scholarship, and objectivity. Avoid a defensive or apologetic tone. Do not use a harsh or abusive tone, especially when referring to a scholar whose argument you want to refute.

Sexism in language should also be eliminated because the world is moving consciously to gender-neutral language. Some researchers, in order to feminize language, resort to quaint coinages like "Chairwoman", Policewoman", "businesswoman", "saleswoman", etc. Such expressions can be replaced with a Chairperson, police officer, business executive, and salesperson. Gendered pronouns should be avoided as much as possible.

Consistency

There is a need to ensure that all elements of research are carried out in a consistent manner. Consistency in spelling has already been pointed out. But that is not the only area where consistency should be ensured. There should be consistency in the use of terminologies and methods of documentation. There should be no movement from one form to another. Also important is consistency is font size, spacing, indenting, setting of margins, page numbering, and use of symbols.

Transitional Connections

There is a need to establish a logical relationship between ideas, sentences, paragraphs, and even chapters. This helps the work to have unity. Examples of appropriate transitional connections are:

1. *For additions* – furthermore, also, in addition, besides
2. *For contrast* – however, on the contrary, in contrast, yet.
3. *For repetition* - in order words, as has been noted, as previously stated.
4. *For alternatives* - either, neither on the other hand, otherwise, conversely.
5. *For exemplification* - for instance, for example.
6. *For comparison* – likewise, in comparison, similarly.
7. *For results* - therefore, consequently, thus, accordingly, thereby, as a result, because.

Checking for Noise

Noise, in communication parlance, is a barrier, a hindrance or anything that impedes effective communication. When this occurs in the research report, it obtrudes. Prominent noise or barriers encountered in revision include confusion in fonts, missing sentences and paragraphs, inappropriate examples and explanations, poor grammar, and significant omissions. These should be carefully detected and appropriately corrected.

Ensuring Appropriate Use of Verbs

The researcher should ensure that the quotations are appropriately introduced. There is a need to ensure that the reader is made aware of who the speaker is, what the quotation refers to, and from where the quotation was lifted. To this end, signal phrases are important.

Signal phrases are used to show the reader that the words or ideas that follow are from another source. Many researchers, especially neophytes, fail to use the appropriate signal phrase to reflect exactly the attitude of the scholar whose material has been quoted. The verb chosen for the signal phrase should, therefore, perfectly indicate the objective of the source being quoted. It is inappropriate to say, for instance, that a scholar is commenting when he is refuting a point. The following are some of the appropriate verbs which the researcher should use to reflect exactly the intention of the scholar being quoted:

Acknowledges	Admits	Agrees
Argues	Asserts	Believes
Claims	Comments	Concedes
Declares	Demonstrates	Emphasizes
Endorses	Illustrates	Implies
Insists	Maintains	Notes
Observes	Points out	Refutes
Reports	Reveals	States
Suggests	Thinks	Writes

The researcher should remember that using the same verb will result in unnecessary repetition. There is a need to vary their placement in order to avoid monotony.

Accuracy of Paraphrases

The aim of a paraphrase is to restate the author's words in your own words. There is a purpose for this. The most prominent reason for paraphrasing is to make the ideas being paraphrased clearer and relate them to the main purpose of the research. As a result, it is good to recreate the order, structure, and emphasis used by the author whose work is being paraphrased by the researcher.

It is acceptable to use brief, direct quotations in your paraphrase if the original words of the author need to be maintained in the paraphrase. In that case, the researcher should ensure that they are indicated with quotation marks.

Final Checking

The researcher should now go back to the preliminary pages to ensure that they logically relate to the rest of the report. It is necessary to ensure that the same font is used throughout the paper, including the preliminary pages.

The title page Is very important to follow the recommendations approved by the institution or granting agency. If the study is in partial fulfillment of the requirements for a degree, this should be stated and in the appropriate way established by the institution and by the particular academic area. The researcher has no right to invent his own method in order to make it more fanciful or to use a different form from that approved by the institution.

Nine

DOCUMENTATION

Critically speaking, the author resides in the imagination of the reader just as the dead person finds existence in the imagination of the living, in an effort to seek meaning out of a sea of meaninglessness, one sometimes craves for explanations, seeking familiar motifs and archetypal symbols through which to explain them.

-Emeka Nwabueze

Visions and Re-visions

When description is just an inventory of sights and sounds, it is not yet an essay. It becomes an essay only when a writer provides an interpretation of the details that catches the reader by surprise.

-James C. Raymond

Definition

Documentation is the process of providing written acknowledgment of the appropriate source of information used in research work. It is not limited to written sources; hence, such other sources are oral interviews, recordings, and television programmes are also supposed to be documented.

Source being documented must be recorded in conventional style to enable the reader to trace them for further study and investigation, where necessary. Careful documental shows the reader how far the researcher has extensively and thoroughly investigated the extent topic.

Systems of Documentation

Systems of documentation have changed from time to time. Because the older system of note citation is still found in books and documents, it is necessary to briefly discuss the system, if only to clarify the difference between the old and new.

Different academic disciplines recommend different styles of documentation, and the researcher is urged to follow the recommended style very faithfully and consistently. This text has attempted to discuss all the relevant styles.

This chapter, therefore, provides a necessary guide to the form of documentation recommended in major academic disciplines. Specifically, the Modern Language Association (MLA) is a system of documentation used mainly in the Arts and Humanities. **The American Psychological Association** (APA) style, which emphasizes author/date system, is mainly used for social science with versions for biological and earth science, education and business. **The Number Systems** (CBE, ACS, AMS, and AIP) are related systems used for the medical sciences, biological and agricultural sciences, and applied sciences. **The Chicago Manuel of Style** (CMS) is a system used for some of the humanities as an alternative to the MLA.

MODERN LANGUAGES ASSOCIATION (MLA)

The older style of documentation adopted by the Modern Language Association is called the note citation. It requires the application of footnotes or endnotes. Incidentally, this method now constitutes part of the recommendation by the Chicago Manual of Style, as will be discussed later in this chapter.

Comment or Content Notes

Content notes also referred to as comment notes, are used to cite sources of information used in a research report, to provide additional information or comments which are not suitable for inclusion in the text of the report, to dirt the reader's attention to other pertinent opinions, and to refer the reader to other pages of the text.

When explanatory comments are added to the note citation to prevent interruption of the flow of the paper, such notes are notes are referred to as content, comment, or substantive notes. Such notes are usually used to explain a term, supply additional examples, refer the reader to another source or acknowledge research. They are also used for further amplification of the information being discussed and sometimes to make digressive comments. The note citation system requires a bibliography at the end of the report.

Parenthetical Citations

This is the most modern system of documentation which began to dominate research since its development and approval by the Modern Language Association in 1984. In this style, references are placed in parentheses within the text rather than in footnotes or endnotes. The parenthetical note then refers the reader to complete bibliographical information on the source, which includes details of publication. This bibliographical information inserted at the end of the paper is labeled Works Cited or Reference List.

The aim of parenthetical documentation requires the abolition of the doubt labour involved in repeating identical information in both the note citation and the bibliography. It stresses only one complete citation and gives the reader a quicker perusal of the source of the citation.

Major Differences

The major changes in documentation style are the elimination of all footnotes and endnotes, the inclusion of parenthetical notes within the text, and the change of the nomenclature of the bibliography section to Works Cited. Other changes are:

(a) The replacement of Roman numerals with Arabic numerals in everything except play titles, as well as on the preliminary pages of the text;
(b) Deletion of p. and pp. (for page and pages) in front of page numbers;
(c) Replacement of 1 or 11 with line or lines until lineation is established in the research report, after which it becomes completely eliminated.
(d) Using a colon rather than a coma to separate volume numbers from page numbers in journal entries;
(e) Elimination of the comma after a journal-title.

In-text Citation

It is necessary to point out that academic areas in the Humanities are not particularly concerned with the date of a scholarly work. Their focus is on the authors and the internal qualities of the publication. This is why MLA recommends that in-text citations should feature mainly the author's name, the title of the publication and the page numbers. Parenthetical references should be quite brief but clear and accurate. The researcher should provide enough information to make it easy for the reader to identify the source in the Works Cited list.

In-text citation is used to indicate that a writer has lifted material from another source. The citation is indicated within the paper and refers the reader to the list of works cited at the end of the paper. In-text citation tells the reader where the borrowed material can be found in the original source. The following are different methods of incorporating in-text citations in the research report.

Introducing an Authority

The first time an authority is introduced in the text, both the first name and the surname of the authority are to be used. Subsequent references should simply refer to the author's surname:

> Damian Opata contends that Soyinka's Elesin Oba is an example of a heroic character (27)

The complete documentation of the source should then be provided in Works Cited. In the subsequent reference to the authority, the writer can simply say:

> Opata further states ….

Identifying the Source

When necessary, it may be helpful to state what gives the source authority and recognition:

> Emmanuel Ezeani, a seasoned professor of Political Economy, suggests that ….

Author and Work

Both the author and the work should be mentioned at the time they are both introduced in order to maintain a smooth rendering of the report. The page numbers should be enclosed in parentheses.

> In the article "Importance of Oral Tradition in Dramatic Study", S.O. Amali maintains that oral tradition is "handed down orally from generation to generation" (5).

Citing More Than One Work by the Same Author

If the researcher refers to more than one work by the same author, he should provide a shortened version of each of the titles in each citation. The Works Cited should then contain the complete documentation of the two references. This is because citing only the author and the page may confuse the reader. The following is an example:

> Sam Onuigbo declared that the study of Stylistics is an important area of English study (Introduction 5). He seems to confirm this view in his study of undergraduate inter-language (Error Analysis 28), where he identifies…..

None mention of Authority

If the authority's name is not mentioned at the beginning of a paraphrase or summary, the authority's name and page reference number should be placed in parenthesis at the end of the statement:

> Nigerian youths migrate to the cities for employment and professional purposes (Ejifor 26).

> Novels by Igbo writers often reveal a "pattern of linguistic regression" (Inyama 120).

If the name of the authority is mentioned in the text, only the page number, placed in parenthesis, should be indicated.

> Nnadozie Inyama argues that novels by Igbo writers often reveal a "pattern of linguistic regression" (120).

More than One Work by the Same Author

If you are citing more than one work by the same author, the shortened title of the work being cited should be used to identify it and separate it from the other sources. Use of comma to separate the name from the shortened title as follows:

> Achebe states that "proverbs are the palm oil with which words are eaten" (*Things Fall Apart* 215)

It is acceptable to shorten *Things Fall Apart* merely as *Things* or use an abbreviation (TFA) to identify it. This applies only to situations where you have cited other material from Chinue Achebe.

Work by Two or Three Authors

If the source being referred to is by two or three authors, the full names of the authors should be mentioned, but subsequent references should merely refer to their surnames alone. Use commas to separate the names of the authors as follows;

> It is important not to ignore the importance of catharsis in elegiac poetry (Onuigbo, Akwanya, and Okoro 36).

> Onuigbo, Akwanya, and Okoro have endorse the importance of catharsis in elegiac poetry (36).

Work by More Than Three Authors

There are two acceptable methods here. First, you can use the names of all the authors not minding the number. Alternatively, you can use the surname of the first author followed by "and others". The Latin words *et alii* (shortened as *et al),* which means "and others," is no longer in vogue.

Work by an Unknown Author

If the author of the work being cited is unknown and used either the complete version in the text or a shortened version in the parenthetical citation. The focus should be on the title and page numbers.

> According to Theories of the Modern Theatre, naturalism can be described as scientific realism (28).

> Naturalism can be described as scientific realism (*Theories 28).*

Work by a Corporate Author

If the source is a corporate publication where individual members of the group are not identified, the corporate name should be used. If the name is long, common abbreviations or acronyms should be used as follows:

> Theatrical performances are already popular among county dwellers (Natl. Assoc. of Theatre Arts Students 3)

Multivolume Work

To cite material from one volume of a source with multivolume, include the volume number, followed by a colon and a space and then add the page number as follows:

Uche Nwaozuzu states that a typical actor suffers from a significant amount of neurosis (4:234).

Poetry, Drama and the Bible

Reference to sources like poetry, drama or the Holy Writ should not stress page numbers but lines, acts and scenes, chapters and verses. This will enable the reader to consult any other edition of the publication order than the one used by the researcher. Reference of the Act, scene or line number should be in Arabic numerals and separated by periods with no space before or after them. Reference to the Bible should be strictly made to chapters and verses. The citation should identify the book of the Bible, the chapter, and the pertinent verse being referred to. The version of the Bible you are using should be mentioned in the first citation, while the book, chapter, and verse should be mentioned in subsequent citations. The names of Biblical books should neither be underlined nor enclosed in quotation marks.

Constitution

When making reference to the Constitution, use common abbreviations as follows:

Constitution	Const.
Article	Art.
Section	Sect.

Quote of a Quote

In the case where the book you are using has lifted a quotation from another source which is unavailable to you, and you want to quote from the source you have perused, begin with the original source, after which the extent source is stated.

> Thomas Ashburn has pointed out that "African drama enjoys an enviable position in the corpus of world dramatic literature" (as qtd. In Furly 382).

The "Work Cited" entry should then contain a full bibliographical entry of Furly's book where the quotation appears, as follows:

Thomas Ashburn, *Miracles in Drama* (London: Heinemann, 1995), p. 48 as cited in Lester Furly, *The Development of Dramatic Art.* (New York: Holman, 2006), 204.

GENERAL GUIDELINES ON CITATION AND BIBLIOGRAPHY FORMAT (WORK CITED)

This is a comprehensive listing of works cited in the text of the research report.

The Author or Editor

The general format is to place the last name of the author before the first and separate them with a comma. Add any middle name or initial after the first name, ensuring that any addition reflects what appears in the book being documented. Indicate the end of this unit of entry with a full stop.

When documenting information from a source written by two or more authors, list the names in the same order used in the title page of the book. The name of the first author is inverted, but the others are not. Separate all the names with commas, and place the word "and" before the final name.

To document a work written by four or more authors, list the names of all the authors or provide just the first person's name in the inverted form and use "and others" after the name.

For corporate or group publication, omit any initial article like *An, A* or *The* from the title of the work.

In the case of a source where an editor or editors are listed, insert the abbreviation *Ed* to represent editor or *Eds* to represent editors.

The Title of the Source

Underline (or place in italics) the titles of books, journals, magazines, newspapers, plays, films and websites. Ensure that all major words in the title are capitalized. The full stop (period) completing this unit of the entry should not be underlined.

If a work has a subtitle, do not ignore it. Use a colon to separate the main title from the subtitle.

Publication Information

If more than one city is listed in the publication data, mention only the first city on the list. Insert a colon after the name of the city. If the city of publication is not properly known, insert the name of country where the work was published after the city' name. The name of the city and the country should be separated with a comma.

It is not necessary to enter the entire name of the publisher, especially if it is long. Provide a shortened form of the publisher's name and place a comma after it. It is best to shorten the publisher's name by simply using the principal name. For instance, rather than insert "Heinemann Educational Books Limited", it is appropriate to simply say "Heinemann". For books published by university presses, the words 'University" and "Press" can be abbreviated. For instance, for a book published by Ibadan University Press, the researcher can simply state Ibadan UP.

Publisher's Imprint

The imprint of a title is usually listed above the publisher's name on the title page. Where they appear together, it is appropriate to list both the publisher's name and an imprint. Use the hyphen to separate the two names.

Copyright Date

The copyright date is either found on the title page or on the copyright page. Sometimes, it may appear in both places. Insert a period after the date.

It is necessary for the researcher to ensure that the information being cited is copied directly from the source to avoid any errors. The following examples are intended to serve as an aid to the researcher.

It is necessary to repeat that all entries should be alphabetized according to the last name of the author.

Book by One Author

Nwoji, Ugochkwu, *The Craft of Engineering*. New York: New York UP., 2007.

Book by Two Authors

Okonta, Anthony I., and Chike Omeje. *Perspectives on Human Resources in the University System*. New York: Random House, 2007.

Book by Three Authors

Ahazuem, Jones, Sam C. Chukwu, and Emeka Okpara. *Introduction to the Humanities.*
 London: Heinemann, 2008.

Book by More Than Three Authors

If a book is written by more than three authors, you may list all the author's names as they appear on the title page or provide the name of the first author and use the words "and others" before the title of the book.

Oyeoku, O.K., Ola Oloidi, Chris Ikwuemsi, and Emeka Nwosu, *studies in Popular Culture.*
 Oxford: Blackwell, 2008.

Oyeoku, O.K., and others. *Studies in Popular Culture.* Oxford: Blackwell, 2008.

More than one book by the same author

If the list of Works Cited contains more than one publication by the same author, there is no need to repeat the name of the author after the first entry. The author's name should be replaced with hyphens followed by a period. The hyphens are meant to represent the exact name of the author.

Okolo, Batho. *Understanding Enzymes.* London: Routledge, 2008.

---------- *Genomics and Environmental Regulation.* New York: New York U.P., 2009.

Book by a Corporate Author

Academy for Performing Arts. *Basic Performance Aesthetics Arima:* UTT Press, 2009.

Anthology

Okafor, Chinyere, Ed. *An Anthology of Humour.* New York, Random House, 2008.

Works in an Anthology

Egwuda, Felix. "Prisoners Come Home" *A Handbook of African Drama,* Ed. C. Amonyeze.
 New York; Norton, 2009.

Introduction, Preface, Foreword, or Afterword to a Book

Nebo, Chinedu O., Foreword, *Alternative for Reluctant Mothers*. By Echi Nwogu, Nsukka: University of Nigeria Press, 2009.

A Work from a Journal Reprinted in a Textbook

Ezeani, Chinwe "Information-seeking behavior of Humanities Librarians". *College Librarian* 20, 4 (2008) 220-36. Rpt. *In Studies in Library Science* Ed. E. Ikegbune, Cambridge: The University Press, 2009.

Translated Book

Aristotle Poetics, Trans, Toni Duruaku. Harmondsworth, Eng.: Penguin, 2007.

DOCUMENTING JOURNAL ARTICLES

A journal is a publication specifically meant for a particular discipline or professional body. It is different from a magazine, which is written for a general audience. Most of the information required for a "Works Cited" entry can be found on the first page of the journal or sometimes in the footer of the article being cited.

A journal article is documented as follows:

(a) *The title of the article:* This should be enclosed in quotation marks with a period inside the closing quotation marks.

(b) *The name of the journal:* This should be underlined or placed in italics. Capitalize the major words in the title of the journal. No period is necessary here.

(c) *Volume and issue numbers:* The volume number of the journal should be provided. If the journal is published with continuous pagination, insert only the volume number after the name of the journal. If the issues of the journal are paginated separately, insert a period after the volume number and add the issue number. Note that in a journal paginated continuously, the number "1" is used to identify only the first page of the first issue in a volume, while the first page of a subsequent issue in that volume is numbered to follow immediately the last page of the first volume. This sequence continues until the volume is exhausted. In a journal paginated separately, the number 1 is used to identify the first page of each issue in a volume.

(d) *Publication date:* The year of publication should be placed in parentheses after the volume or issue number. For a magazine or newspaper entry, the date of issue should be provided immediately after the name of the magazine or newspaper. The day should be followed by the month, Abbreviate the months except for May, June, and July, which are usually not abbreviated. Finally, state the year of publication.

(e) *Page numbers:* A colon should be used to separate the date from the page number. The inclusive page numbers of the article should be stated. This means all the pages should be separated with a hyphen. For page numbers that have the same hundreds or thousands of digits, it is not necessary to repeat the digit when listing the inclusive page numbers. For instance, rather than stating 223-239, you should merely state 223-39. For magazine and newspaper articles where an article starts on one page and continues on another or other pages, insert only the first-page number followed by a plus a follows: 28 + for an article which started on page 28 and continued on other pages.

The following examples are intended to assist the researcher in preparing appropriate Works Cited documentation.

Scholarly Article in a Journal

Eze, Ada M. "The Art of Dramatic Art" Journal of Contemporary Theatre 42(2008): 231-39.

When citing information from a journal paginated separately, include the issue number as well, as follows:

Igwe, Charles A. "Serendipity Plants". *International Journal of Agriculture* 32.1 (2000: 106-15.

Article in a Monthly Magazine

Nnanna, Ndubisi, "in search of African Theatre". Newswatch Jan. 2009: 27-32.

Article in a Weekly Magazine

Onyeji, Christian. "Understanding India Music" *New Yorker* 5 Jan. 2009: 28-32.

Article in a Daily Newspaper

Agbo, Ben. "Managing a new Programme" New Times 12 Feb. 2009, Sec. 3:4+.

Editorial in a Newspaper

Offiah, Veronica. "Environmental Factors in Nutrition. "Editorial. *New York Times* 22 July 2009.

Book or Film Review in a Journal

For a book or film review, the following method should apply: start with the name of the reviewer and the title of the review (if any). State that it is a review by using the abbreviated phrase, Rev. of, then the title of the work being reviewed, and finally the name of the author, editor or director in case of a film. The following example gives a title to the review of a film. Follow the same method for the review of a book.

Ugwu, Ifeanyi. "Paternal Love". Rev. of *My Father's Love,* dir. Obi Okoli, *Nsukka Journal of the Humanities 8* (2009): 62-66.

REFERENCE WORKS

There is no need for full bibliographical information for renowned reference works like the Encyclopedia, Dictionary or Glossaries because the entries in them are organized alphabetically. The common method is to list the author's name (if stated), the title of the article, the name of the reference work, the edition, and the year of publication.

Encyclopedia Article

"Classical Drama". *The New Encyclopedia Britannica. 22nd ed. 2008.*

Dictionary Entry

Advanced Learner's Dictionary. 7th ed. 2009.

Government Publications

Government publications are usually printed by the Government Printer, and this should be noted, but there could be exceptions. In citing a government publication, start with the name of the issuing government agency. The title of the work should be underlined, and the city of publication should be clearly indicated as follows:

Government of the Republic of Trinidad and Tobago, Public Relations Office. *A Guide a Sources of Information.* Port-of-Spain: Government Printer, 2008.

Documenting a Law Case

In the case of the law case, state the name of the first plaintiff, the first defendant, and the case number. Use the abbreviation v. (which stands for versus) to separate the name of the first plaintiff and first defendant. Also, use the abbreviation *No.* (for number) before the case number. Include the name of the deciding court and the date of the decision. Note that law cases should be underlined in the text of the paper but should not be underlined in the Work Cited.

Thesis or Dissertation

To document a thesis or dissertation, start with the name of the researcher, the title of the thesis or dissertation, the name of the university granting the degree, the date of completion and other publication information. Use the abbreviation Diss (standing for dissertation) in the case of a dissertation entry.

>Jackson, Michael. "Differing Perception of Musical Lyrics". Diss. Ohio: Bowling Green State University, 2006.

Play Performance

>The Dragon's Funeral By Emeka Nwabueze. Dir. Uche Nwaozuzu. National Theatre, Lagos. 12 Jan. 2009.

Lecture

In the case of a lecture, either a public lecture or a class lecture, the important thing is to identify the site and date of the lecture. State the title of the lecture and, if possible, the kind of lecture it is. It is necessary for the researcher to give all the necessary information that would help the reader to know how to obtain a copy of the lecture.

>Modum, Paul E. "Harnessing Literature". Faculty of Arts Lecture Series. New Arts Theatre. University Nigeria, Nsukka. 10 Oct. 2009.

Oral Interview

When documenting an oral interview conducted by the researcher, the most important information is the name of the person interviewed and the date of the interview. If the interview was conducted by another person other than the researcher, the name of the interviewer and the title of the interview (if any) should be clearly stated.

>Uchenna Anyanwu. Personal Interview. Oct. 22 2008.

Radio or Television Programme

If the reference is to a specific episode, use quotation marks to indicate the title and underline the title. If there is a specific presenter, start the entry with the name of the presenter. There is no need to indicate the time of the programme.

Adirika, Amobi, African Dances. ABS Awka, 13 June 2008.

ONLINE BOOKS, ARTICLES, AND DOCUMENTS

To determent online publications, start with the title of the Internet site, the date of publication and the organization sponsoring the site. This is usually found at the bottom of the homepage. Use the most recent update of the material. Provide the complete URL (Internet address or the Web site), the access identifier (http, ftp, telnet, news), appropriate punctuation marks, and both path and file names to enable the reader to locate the source. The address should be placed within angle brackets (< >) and separate clearly from other punctuation marks in the citation. Double-check the URLs on your list in case of a change in the Internet address. To avoid the possibility of the disappearance of the site, it is advisable for the researcher to print out a hard copy of the material used in the research.

Electronic Book

Okpoko, Alex, *Foundations of Archaeology*. 2007. 20 June 2009. http://www.umich.edu/.

Web Site

Nwadialo, B-Shaw. *Nigeria Customs Handbook.* 7 Aug. 2008. UNILAG. 12 Apri. 2009. http://cuwebi.html.custums.org.

Personal Home Page

Ezenwaka, Chidum. Home page. 5 Feb. 2009 www.ezenwaka.com.

CD-ROM

To cite a CD-ROM, you should indicate the part of the CD-ROM being cited and then provide the title of the CD. You should start the entry with the name of the author if provided.

Ohiaeriaku, Tasia. "Towards the Rising Sun" Database of Contemporary Short Plays on CD-ROM. CD-ROM. Nsukka: UNN Library, 2009.

E-mail

To document an e-mail entry, start with the name of the person who created the mail. Identify the recipient of the mail by stating E-mail to if you are the recipient of the email, use the words the *author* rather than your name.

Diala, Isidore, "Re: Academy for the Performing Arts Seminar". E-mail to Stephen Paul. 24 May 2009.

AMERICAN PSYCHOLOGICAL ASSOCIATION (APA)

This style of documentation was established by the American Psychological Association. The Association publishes a style of documentation entitled *Publication Manual of the American Psychological Association*. This style, like the MLA, also favours the use of parenthetical citations within the text of the research report. The major difference, however, is that while the MLA recommends mentioning the author and work, the APA recommends that the author and date should be mentioned. That is why this style of documentation is also called *the author-date system*.

It is the view of the American Psychological Association that the date of publication of scientific research is very crucial, hence the recommendation that the date should be placed in parenthesis immediately after the author is mentioned. The only exception to this rule is the content note.

The reference list represents all the works cited in the research paper.

In-text Citation

In the APA style of documentation, the in-text citations mainly insert the last name of the author of the source being cited and the year of publication of the source. If quotations are used in the paper, the page numbers from where the quotations were extracted should be specified by the researcher. These should be preceded with the abbreviation p. (for the page from where the quotation was extracted) or pp. (representing the pages) from where the quotation was made if it is more than one page. The reader is expected to identify the work by looking for the title of the work in the bibliography at the end of the paper. The following are examples of in-text citations.

Work by a Single Author

In documenting a work by a single author, insert the name of the author and the year of publication of the work at the appropriate point in the paper, as follows:

In a previous study (Chineme, 2008), caged animals were......

If the author's name appears as an integral part of the sentence, only the year of publication should be enclosed in parenthesis as follows:

Chineme (2008) concluded that caged animals....

If there is a need to mention the page in the in-text citation, the following method is appropriate:

Chineme (2008, p. 17) concluded that caged animals .....

Where both the name of the author and the date of publication appear in the textual discussion, do not bother to enclose anything in parenthesis, thus:

In 2008, Chineme studied the temper of caged animals in relation to .....

If subsequent references are made to the same study within the same paragraph, the year of publication should not be enclosed in parenthesis. However, the researcher needs to ensure that the study being referred to cannot be confused with other studies in his research report, thus:

In a more recent study, Madukwe (2008) discovered that caged animals are susceptible to fatigue Madukwe also suggested.

Work by Two Authors

Since scientific research usually involves teamwork, multiple authorship is commonly reflected in most sources. The names of the authors and the date of publication should be mentioned each time such works are referred to thus:

In a more recent study, Nzewi and Ohuche (2007) found out...

OR

Early development of children is determined by the nature of their early parental management (Nzewi & Ohuche, 2007).

It is acceptable to use an ampersand (&) to separate the names of the authors.

Work by More Than Two Authors

Mention the names of the three authors thus:

In recent study (Ozioko, Ukwueze & Onuoha)....

For works by more than three authors, mention the names of all the authors the first time the reference occurs. In subsequent citations, give the surname of the first author followed by the words *et al.* ("and others") and insert the date of publication. Note that et al. should neither be italicized nor underlined and that there should be no period after the word "et".

For works with six or more authors, mention only the last name of the first author, followed by et al., even in the first citation of the work.

Authors with the Same Surname

If two or more authors with the same surname are cited, include the initials of the authors in all citations irrespective of whether or not the publication date differs thus:

Interesting results of the polls were reported by A Dike (1999) and K. O. Dike (1982)...

Same Author and Publication Date

If there are different works by the same author that have the same publication date, identify the works by "a", "b", and "c", as the case may be, thus:

Oluikpe (1999a, 2004b and 2008c) discusses...

Two or More Works by Different Authors in the Same Citation

If two or more works by different authors appear in the same parenthetical citation, arrange them in alphabetical order and use a semicolon to separate the citations thus:

Studies show that aspirin is sometimes taken in unusually large doses (Aka, 2008; Okezie, 2009).

Personal Communication

Personal communications are letters, memos, personal interviews, telephone conversations, and e-mail messages which the researcher used in the course of the research. These sources should be cited in the text only; they should not appear in the reference list.

REFERENCE LIST

The APA recommends that the Reference List should be started on a new page ad centred on the page, about one inch from the top of the page. The entries should be listed in alphabetical order by the author's last name. The reference list should contain only those sources explicitly cited in the research paper, with the exclusion of personal communication, in the case of sources with more than one author, alphabetized by the last name of the first author.

If an author's name appears as the first name in a single-author source as well as the first name in a multiple-author source, list the one in which he appears as a single author before the multiple-author source.

In a situation where more than one work by one author was cited, arrange the works according to their date of publication. The entry with the earliest date should be listed first.

If there are two or more works by the same author published on the same date, arrange the titles in alphabetical order according to the first important word in each title. Add the letters a, b, c, d, and so on to the date of publication to distinguish the works from each other.

The first line of each entry should be flushed with the left margin, and subsequent lines should be indented one-half inch or five spaces in a hanging indent.

The reference list should be written in the following order: name(s) of the author(s) should be in inverted order, the year of publication should be placed in parenthesis, the title of publication should be underlined or placed in italics, and finally, list the place of publication and the name of the publisher. The publisher's name should be listed in the brief form. For instance, instead of writing "Evans Brothers Nigeria Publishers Limited, it is accepted to simply write Evans.

The following is a sample bibliographical listing:

Book by a Single Author

Muoneke, N.E. (2005). *Measuring Animal Intelligence through Mathematical Equations*. London: Longman.

Book by Two or More Authors

Okeke F. N., Onwurah, A.E. & Ene-Obong, H.N (2007). *Scientific Analysis*. Ibandan: Macmillan.

In the case of a book with a new edition, identify the edition in parentheses immediately after the title. If the book is edited, simply add Ed or Eds after the name(s) of the editor(s.

Chapter in a Book

Eze, N.O. (2008). Mathematical Characterization. In Mbanefo, G. (Ed.) *Contemporary Discourses (*pp. 255-275). London: Blackwell.

Journal Articles

To document journal articles, APA recommends that the researcher should start with the author's last name and follow with initials. Use a common to separate the last name from the first name and/or initials. If there is two to six authors, invert the last names and initials of all authors. Use a comma to separate names from initials and use an ampersand (&) in addition to a comma before the last name of the last author. The year of publication should be enclosed in parentheses. If the entry involves a magazine issue on a specific day or month, give the year of the publication followed by the month (and day, if necessary).

Note that the title of the article in a journal is not enclosed in quotation marks and that only the first word is capitalized. Underline (or place in italics) the name of the journal or magazine, and capitalize the first word of the title and any proper nouns. When citing an article from a journal paginated continuously, provide only the volume number in italics. When citing from a journal paginated separately, include the issue number of parentheses as well as the volume number. Only the volume number is italicized.

Hereunder is an example of the citation method for a journal article by a single author.

Onuoha, M.K. (2007). Towards a new analysis of African rocks. *Journal of Geophysics,* 26(1), 66-78.

Film

In a film citation, give the name of the producer and the director simultaneously. Include their titles in parentheses. Give the date of production (also in parentheses) and the title of the film, specifying the medium to prevent the reader from confusing it without another medium, thus:

Nnamdi, Andy (Producer). & Udengwu, E. (Director). (2006). *Guardian of the Cosmos* (Film) Nsukka: University of Nigeria.

Legal References

Because of the complexity of legal references, a researcher whose work involves intricate law references should consult. A *Uniform System of Citation,* published by Harvard Law Review Association. If the researcher's legal citations are references to court cases and statutes, the following order should be followed:

Court Cases

Citations to court decisions should follow the following order:

(a) Names of the plaintiff(s) and the defendant(s) with the word "versus separating them, and summarized as vs;
(b) State the volume, name and page of the law report being cited;
(c) State (in parentheses) the name of the court that decided the case.

Statutes

When citing from commonly known laws, the following format should be used:

(a) Cite the applicable constitution;
(b) State the article;
(c) State the section where it appears.

Internet Sources

While citing from the internet, the following information should be included:

(1) *Internet Address* – State a stable Internet address which should direct the reader to the work. If the work has a digital object identifier (DOI), this should be used. If there is none, use a stable URL. If the URL is unstable as is sometimes the case with online newspapers and some subscription-based databases, use the home page of the site.

The researcher should realize that reputable scholarly publishers now assign a DOI to journal articles and other documents. The DOI is a unique alphanumeric string assigned by a registration agency and the purpose is to identify content and provide a link to its location on the Internet.

(2) *Retrieval Date* – Where a work is finalized the date like a journal article, use the date within the body of the citation. If the work is not dated and may be subject to change often, as is the case with online encyclopedia articles, state the date the information was retrieved. Note that the date of the retrieved of an electronic source is very important because the content being cited may be changed or updated. This offers the reader information on the content of the material at the time of the research.

THE NUMBER SYSTEMS

The number system was established by the Council of Science Editors (CSE), formerly known as the Council of Biology Editors (CBE). The CSE/CBE manual titled *Scientific Style and Format: The CBE Manual for Authors, Editors, and Publishers* gives general information on documentation as well as the conventions for the use of chemical names and formulas.

The manual also presents two formats for citing and documenting research sources. They are referred to as the citation-sequence system and the name-year system. Specifically, the Number System requires the researcher to use an in-text number rather than the year and a list of references that are numbered either alphabetically or in the order in which they appear in the text.

There are three basic requirements of the system:

1. Each system requires the inclusion of a list of references with a number assigned to each entry. The list may either be presented alphabetically and numbered consecutively or arranged and numbered in the consecutive order in which the references are cited in the research report.
2. For in-text citations, appropriate numbers are used and these are usually inserted at the end of the summary, paraphrase, or direct quotation. The in-text references vary. They could either be stated in superscripts or parentheses. The numbers can also be inserted in boldface. The researcher may include the name of the authority in the text, but it is the number that serves as the main reference to the source.

3. When a direct quotation is made by the researcher, he should state the number of the source and the specific page number from where the citation was lifted.

Researchers using the Number Systems should note that the title of the list of references is stated according to the subject area. For instance, the references for agriculture are titled *References,* while those for Astronomy or Geology are titled *Literature Cited.* References for research conducted in Biology, Botany and Zoology are titled *Cited References.*

The Medical Sciences generally use the CBE numbering system or standards established by the *AMA Stylebook/Editorial Manual,* and others. The main recommendation of these sources is that references to the source may be cited through one of the following:

(a) Inserting a superscript number;
(b) Inserting a parenthesized number;
(c) Inserting a bracketed number.

Specific Method

It is necessary to note that different journals specifically state the method to be used in documentation. The specification is usually taken from one of the three methods stated above. The examples are stated below:

Malaria is indirectly linked with high blood pressure[1]

Malaria is indirectly linked with high blood pressure (1).

Malaria is indirectly linked with high blood pressure /1/.

Computer Science uses mainly the CBE style. In-text references to the source may be cited by using superscript number or by parenthesized number. Either of them is acceptable.

Computer database is more useful in scientific research (4).

Computer database is more useful in scientific research[4]

In the CBE Style of documentation recommended for Computer Science, all references should be called in numerical order and listed in the order of the text reference. The list should be given the title "Works Cited". Numbers should be used, followed by periods. The second ad consecutive lines should not be indented, as exemplified in the following journal entry.

Ikekeonwu, G.A.M. "Computing Ideas for students."

Journal of Computing 22 (Jan. 2009), 25-34.

In Chemistry, the ACS Style is quite prominent as a documentary style. In-text references to the source should be cited in one of the following ways:

1. Using the superscript number,
2. Using parenthesized number;
3. Using the author name and date.

Examples are stated as follows:

Patterns of research in oxygen have already been investigated[2]

Patterns of research in oxygen have already been investigated (3)

Patterns of research in oxygen have already been investigated (Okafor et al., 2009)

The bibliography style for the ACS recommends that all references are collated in numerical order if cited by number. Alternative, it can also be collated in alphabetical order if the researcher has cited by author. The title of the bibliography section should be "References". Each number entry is listed and numbered in the order in which it appears in the text. When using numbers, they should be placed in parentheses before the source. If the source is a journal article, omit the titles of the articles. The date of the periodicals should be typed in boldface, and the second and consecutive lines should not be indented.

Nwosu, A.K. Organic Chem. 2008, 67-84.

The Department of **Mathematics** uses the AMS Style of documentation. For in-text references, the in-text citation number should be placed within brackets and typed in boldface.

The results of the boundedness theory [2] in mathematical equations state…

The bibliography style recommended for AMS documentation method recommends that all references should be collated in numerical order if the citation is by number or arranged in alphabetical order if the citation is by author. The bibliography list should be given the title References. Each entry should be numbered in the order in which they appear in the text if the researcher is not using the alphabetical arrangement. The titles of books are underlined, and the name of the publisher comes before the city of publication. There is no need to list the specific pages of books.

For journal articles, the title of the article should be inserted in italics. The journal volume number should be put in boldface, immediately followed by the year of publication inserted in parentheses, while the titles of the journals should not be italicized.

Ekwue, Edwin Ikenna, *Linear algebra,* John Wiley, London, 2008.

J.O.C Ezeilo, *The boundedness theory of mathematical equations,* Int. J. Math. **46** (1982), 76-82.

In **Physics and Engineering,** the AIP style is widely accepted. Different styles are used by the different journals, and the researcher is advised to consult appropriate journals for the style they use. Generally, in-text citation involves the use of superscript numbers.

For the bibliography, the references are collated in the order in which they appear in the text, with the insertion of superscript numbers. Titles of books are inserted in italics. The name of the publisher comes before the place of publication. It is necessary to provide specific page references. If the reference is to a journal, the title of the article should be omitted. The title of the journal should be abbreviated but not italicized or underlined. The volume number is inserted in boldface, followed by page numbers. Finally, the year of publication is inserted in parentheses immediately after the page numbers.

P.N. Okeke and F.N. Okeke, Contemporary Physics (Wiley, London, 2006), p. 28.

C. Ubachukwu, Int. J. Phys. **22,** 56-64, (2008).

Summary

The following is the general summary for preparing appropriate documentation under the Number Systems. This is only the general method, as the peculiarities of each academic area have already been discussed.

Citation Sequence for In-text Citations

1. Insert the superscript number ***immediately*** after a source is mentioned or each time a material is cited from the source. This number should correspond to the number assigned to that particular source on the reference list.

2. The numbers should be assigned according to the sequence in which the sources are introduced in the research report. For instance:

    Uzoegwu[1] and Uzuegbunam[2] have painstakingly argued…

3. In a situation where a phrase makes reference to more than one source, commas should be used to separate the corresponding numbers. There should be no space after each comma, and the numbers should be in superscript. If there is a sequence between two numbers, an en-dash should be used to show that, thus:

    Studies by the Nsukka school[1,2,3-5]…

Citation Sequence for In-text Citation Using Name-Year Method

1. Insert the author's last name and the year of publication in parentheses immediately after the source is mentioned. The use of the author's last name enables the reader to find the corresponding entry on the reference list.

    In a recent analytical study (Uche 2008)

2. If the author's name appears in the text preceding it, the name should not be repeated:

    Uche's analytical study (2008) underscores…….

3. Multiple citations within a set of parentheses should be separated with semicolons; if the year of publication is the same, these citations should be ordered alphabetically, but if they differ, the citations should be ordered chronologically.

In the following studies (Agu 2009; Duraku 2009)

In the following studies (Duruaku 2007; Agu 2009)

Preparing a Reference List

1. Insert the heading "**References**" or "**References Cited**" next to the left margin. The inverted commas should not be inserted.
2. Researchers using the citation-sequence method should list the sources in the order in which they were introduced in the text.
3. In the case of the name-year method, the reference list should be arranged in alphabetical order, starting with the author's last name.
4. In the name-year method, insert the date of publication after the author's name; in the citation-sequence method, the date of publication should be inserted after the name of

the publisher for book entries. In the case of journal articles, the date should be inserted after the name of the journal.

CHICAGO MANUAL OF STYLE (CMS)

The University of Chicago, in an effort to bring more innovation into methods of documentation, published The Chicago Manual of Style. This document provides guidelines for writers in the Arts and Humanities particularly. The main recommendation of the manual is the system of documentation, which allows the researcher either to use footnotes or endnotes and, in some cases bibliography. Some of these recommendations have already been abrogated by the Modern Languages Association documentation style.

The Chicago Manual of Style recommends that in-text citations should take the form of sequential numbers generally described as footnotes or listed at the end of the entire paper and referred to as endnotes. If the paper contains a bibliographical list of all the sources used in the research, the notes should be condensed or shortened to include only the author's last name, the shortened title, and the relevant page numbers.

In-text Citations

For in-text citations, the superscript is used along with Arabic numerals. The superscript numeral should be placed at the end of the quotation or a paraphrase, and the number should follow immediately. There should be no space after the final word or punctuation mark.

Footnotes and Endnotes

Footnotes, usually inserted at the bottom of each page of the research report, and endnotes, usually inserted at the end of each chapter or at the end of the entire report, require superscript numbers within the text and subsequent documentary information. The notes are numbered consecutively by Arabic numerals throughout the paper. The Arabic numerals are elevated one-half space above the line and are placed very close to the end of the material cited. It indicates the full name of the author (as it appears in the source), the title of the publication, the facts of the publication, and the page number or numbers on which the information appears. The first line of each note is indented five spaces. The notes are separated from the text of the research by a double space.

Creating the Superscript

With the evolution of the computer it is no longer a difficult process to create a superscript number as it was during the advent of the typewriter. To create a superscript number, the researcher using Microsoft Word should highlight the number, pull down the menu for Format, click on Font, place a checkmark next to the superscript and click OK.

Preparing Footnotes on CMS Format

If the researcher is using a word-processing outfit, it will automatically design the footnote for your paper. Microsoft word appears quite easier because the researcher should merely pull down the Insert menu and choose Footnote, and a superscript number will appear at the appropriate position.

A researcher using a manual typewriter should leave enough space for footnotes at the bottom of the page to which the reference is being made. It is necessary to create a separator by typing a solid line that stretches across one-third of the page.

Each note should be started with a full-size number. This is followed by a period and a space.

The first line of a note should be indented five spaces. Use single space within a footnote and double space between footnotes. Bibliography is not necessary if the footnotes provide complete bibliographic information for all the sources cited in the research report.

The Chicago Manual of Style allows the use of Ibid to serve as an indication that the source cited in a particular entry is the same as the one in the preceding entry. If the page numbers differ from those in the other entry, the page numbers should be clearly stated.

Preparing Endnotes

The endnotes should be placed on a separate page. The word "Notes" should be centred at the top of the page. The first line of a note should be indented five spaces.

Single space should be used between the lines of an endnote, while double space should be used between entries. As stated above, if the endnotes provide complete bibliographic information for all the sources cited in the paper, there will be no need for a bibliography, and this will constitute unnecessary repetition.

Use the abbreviation Ibid exactly as stated above.

Preparing a Bibliography

A bibliography is necessary for the CMS system only if the notes do not contain complete bibliography information of all the cited sources. If a bibliography is needed, it should be started on a separate page. The word "Bibliography" (without the inverted commas) should be centred at the top of the page. It is also acceptable for the researcher to use "Work Cited" (without inverted commas).

Each entry in the bibliography should be alphabetical according to the last name of each author. If the source has more than one author, alphabetized the last name of the first author.

If the same source is repeated in an entry, there is no need to repeat the author's name. This information can be given by placing the name or names of the author(s) in about seven consecutive dashes.

The second and subsequent lines of every entry should be indentified five spaces, and single-space should be used between the line of an entry. Double-space should separate each entry.

SUMMARY: GENERAL HINTS ON DOCUMENTATION

The researcher should take note of the following information as a guide to appropriate documentation. However, it is necessary to use the method allowed in the particular academic discipline unless the researcher is allowed free use of any documentation method.

Consistency is very important in documentation. Do not mix one method with another. This chapter tried to cover most of the methods of documentation. It is the duty of the researcher to identify the one recommended in his area of research and follow it faithfully. Inability to document properly is usually penalized.

Punctuation

Punctuation marks are used to clarify the meaning of quotations and citations. Their common uses in documentation are summarized as follows:

(a) Use a colon to separate volume numbers form page numbers in a parenthetical citation.
(b) Use of comma to separate the author's name from the title when listing both in a parenthetical citation.

(c) Use a comma to indicate that page or line numbers are not sequential.

(d) Use a hyphen to indicate a continuous sequence of pages or lines.

(e) Use ellipses to indicate an omission within a quotation.

(f) Use a period to spate acts, scenes and lines of dramatic works as well as chapters from verses in Biblical citations.

(g) Use question marks in two distinct ways. When placed inside the final quotation marks, it indicates that the quotation is a question. When placed outside the final quotation marks, the meaning is that the quotation is part of a question posed by the researcher.

(h) Use square brackets to enclose words that have been added to the quotation as a form of clarification, not part of the quoted material.

Placement of In-text Citation

Sometimes, you may need to acknowledge a source not by quotation, which requires inverted commas, but through paraphrase, especially when you have faithfully paraphrased the words of an author. In such a situation, place the author's name and the relevant page number in parenthesis directly after the information used, preferably at the end of the sentence before the final punctuation mark. Parenthetical citation can also be placed earlier in a sentence as an indication that only that part of the sentence contains borrowed material.

Lengthy Quotations

When a quotation occupies more than four continuous lines, set it off from the rest of the text by indenting all the lines one inch or ten spaces from the left margin. Ensure that the first line is not indented further than the others. The entire quotation should be in double-line spacing. If the lengthy quotation occupies more than one paragraph, indent the first line of each paragraph an extra quarter of an inch or three spaces to show the separation of the paragraphs.

Missing Information

Sometimes, a publication used by the researcher may contain missing information. This is common, especially with older publications or special-purpose publications like brochures and pamphlets. These sources may not include all the standard information necessary for appropriate documentation. To ameliorate this, check the library card for the missing information. If it does not contain the information there are conventional ways of documenting sources with missing information.

1. *No Author* - If the author's name is not given in the source being documented, simply omit it and begin the notation with the title of the book or article. Do not use the abbreviation anon.
2. *No Date* - If there is no date in the source being documented, use the abbreviation n.d. in the position where the date would normally appear.
3. *No Publisher or Place of Publication* – When there is no publisher or place of publication in the source, the conventional method is to use the abbreviation n.p. to indicate this. This should be inserted in the position where the publisher and place of publication would normally appear.
4. *No Pagination* – If the pages of the publication are not numbered, use the abbreviation n.pag in the position where the page numbers would normally appear.

PLAGIARISM

Education without morality is like a man with an amputated heart. It is useless to educate a person who has no heart for truth because education makes a good man better and a bad man worse.

- **Emeka Nwabueze, Guardian of the Cosmos,**

Human knowledge is, by definition, that which is unrealizable, that which rules out any possibility of totalizing what it knows or of eradicating its own ignorance.

- **Shoshana Felman.**

Origin

The word plagiarism comes from the Latin word "plagiarus", which means abductor. Abduction, on the other hand, is the act of taking something away from the owner unlawfully by fraud or force. It was originated by the poet, Martial, who called another poet an abductor for having presented his (Martial's) poem as belonging to him. Marshal's use of the word "abductor" to refer to the plagiarist of his poem lays bare the gravity of plagiarism as a literary offence.

A plagiarist Is equal to an offender or a thief. This is because knowledge and creativity are acquired through individual efforts and exertion of energy; hence, ideas, thoughts and expressions which constitute this knowledge become the intellectual property of the person who generated it. If one makes use of these ideas without due acknowledgement, it amounts to literary robbery.

Meaning of Plagiarism

Plagiarism involves a deceptive handling of information a false presentation of ideas acquired in the course of research. It involves the act of taking other people's writings, ideas, thoughts and expressions and passing them off as one's own, and is applicable to both published and unpublished works. It ranges from written or spoken words, from whole documents and paragraphs to sentences and even phrases, as well as statistics, laboratory results, and artwork. It is a kind of deception, fraud and a dishonest misrepresentation of information.

Research is not a process of concealing information but a careful way of acknowledging the sources of any outside information used in the research. For research to retain its academic value, it must be honest especially in the acknowledgement of external sources used. Plagiarism in research is, therefore, not only dishonest but constitutes a kind of self-denial in the sense that the plagiarist denies himself the opportunity to develop as a scholar.

Plagiarism involves double negative attributes. It encompasses the process of stealing, the incidence of deception, and the ethical violation of intellectual property. So, a plagiarist is both a thief and a deceiver. Vincent Ryan Ruggirio illustrates the gravity of the crime of plagiarism in the following words:

Once ideas are put into words and published, they become "intellectual property," and the author has the same rights over them as he or she has over a material possession such as a house or a car. The only real difference is that intellectual property is purchased with mental effort rather than money. Anyone who has ever wracked their brain trying to solve a problem or trying to put an idea into clear and meaningful words can appreciate how difficult mental effort can be. (25).

Intentional and Unintentional Plagiarism

Plagiarism is applicable to both published and unpublished material, including ideas obtained from lectures and classroom assignments. A researcher can plagiarize intentionally of unintentionally. Plagiarism is considered intentional when the plagiarist deliberately passes off another person's original work, ideas, thoughts, phrases, sentences, or even paragraphs as his own. It is considered a deliberate act.

To clarify this issue appropriately, it is necessary to lay bare what constitutes intentional plagiarism:

1. Purchasing a paper from an establishment that is in the business of writing and selling these materials to students;

2. Recycling another student's previously submitted thesis or dissertation;

3. Purchasing a paper from the Internet;

4. Downloading a paper from the Internet;

5. Refusal to document information that neither constitutes the researcher's idea nor belongs to the realm of common knowledge;

6. Using the exact words of another author without enclosing them in quotation marks;

7. Using direct quotations from another author without providing the necessary parenthetical references;

8. Using paraphrase, direct or indirect quotations from published or unpublished work of another person without appropriate documentation.

Many inexperienced researchers indulge in unintentional plagiarism, especially during the process of paraphrasing the material by merely changing a few words in the original and presenting them as his own; he is also guilty of plagiarism, even when he thinks he did not do it intentionally. Even if he writes the borrowed material in his own words, he still needs to acknowledge the source of the material, which is someone else's intellectual property. Failing to do that amounts to plagiarism.

Two major factors may contribute to unintentional plagiarism. The first is when the researcher is unable to differentiate between his own ideas and the ones copied from a book due to a bad method of note-taking. It is, therefore necessary to start right from the note-taking period to differentiate between the researcher's own words and the exact words copied from the book he is using. The second is a slavish adherence to another author's method of handling the subject. This can be done by reproducing the order of ideas, and pattern of presentation observed in the sources being used.

The worst kind of plagiarism, categorized as crassest, is the act of submitting another person's work, purchasing a research paper from one of the companies who perform such dishonest jobs, or presenting as one's own original work thesis or dissertation written by another person. A researcher who relies too much on sources, who fails to form his own ideas from the main bulk of the work, is guilty of unintentional plagiarism. A good researcher should make his own deductions from the material consulted and not rely almost solely on other people's views or postulations.

Reasons for Plagiarism

People plagiarize for a multitude of reasons. Deliberate plagiarism can be inspired by the desire to impress the reader.

This desire may be caused by a lack of adequate vocabulary or ideas on the part of the researcher. A researcher who lacks a good command of the English language can easily be tempted to use the words, phrases, or sentences of another author whose construction of ideas he admires.

Another reason for plagiarism is the fear of scoring a low mark in the paper. This fear is common with lazy students who have not read widely enough to acquire adequate knowledge in their area of investigation. Because of their scanty knowledge of the research area, such researchers find it easier and less tasking to copy other people's work, even that of a fellow student, and submit them as theirs. Since research entails a deep probe into the unknown in order to generate new knowledge, a researcher who lacks the understanding of the state of scholarship in his area of investigation may engage in fraudulent practices like copying already written papers or contracting people to write for them.

Sometimes, when students copy from theses or dissertations already submitted for the award of a degree, they inherit the errors of the author and make worse grades than they could have made if they had painstakingly done the research themselves. Theses and dissertations submitted do not contain the scores given to them. So the lazy student may just be copying from a work that scored a very low grade.

A researcher can also plagiarize due to carelessness. This unintentional plagiarism results from a careless method of taking notes. A researcher who fails to keep a careful record of all the sources of his research material during the note-taking stage may later find it hard to arrange the material accordingly. Not wanting to leave out any plausible material which he considers very important in the development of the work, he may easily fall into the temptation of recording everything as his idea.

Ignorance can also be responsible for unintentional plagiarism. A researcher can unconsciously plagiarize if he cannot distinguish between material that should be acknowledged and that which does acknowledged. Not require

Penalty for Plagiarism

It is necessary to underscore the major reasons that amplify the need to penalize the plagiarist. A researcher who fails to acknowledge the source of material of which he is not the originator and which does not belong to the realm of common knowledge is dishonest. By concealing the source of borrowed information and passing it off as one's own, the researcher is being deceitful.

Plagiarism is illegal and infringes on the copyright law, which invests on the author of a work with the sole right of ownership of the work. By this law any person using the material or information contained therein must obtain permission from the author or at least acknowledge the source. Failure to do this is actionable and can attract litigation from the author.

Like all offences plagiarism attracts punishment. A student who plagiarizes, for instance, may be penalized by being failed in the paper or in the entire course. If plagiarism occurs in a thesis or dissertation, the work may be rejected, and the student asked to engage on a new investigation.

In fact, the common penalty for plagiarism occurring in an institution of higher learning is that the student may be sent on probation if the plagiarism is minimal, or face total rustication from the school if the plagiarism is considered intentional. Whether intentional or unintentional, plagiarism is a punishable offence.

On a more general level, a plagiarist, once discovered, loses the respect of the reader. By plagiarizing, the researcher is indirectly showing the examiner or the reader that he is incapable of handling the research topic. By plagiarizing, the researcher succeeds in cheating himself because he is denying Himself the opportunity to learn. He should consider the fact that if other people had been copying before him, there will be a complete negation of the inflow of ideas, and consequently innovative knowledge.

Methods of Avoiding Plagiarism

To avoid plagiarism the researcher should acknowledge any outside material other than common knowledge. However, some researchers find it difficult to identify what constitutes common knowledge. The following should constitute common knowledge:

1. ***Information known to everyone*** – Information regarded as common knowledge includes birth and death dates of famous individuals, dates of historical, political and literary events, statistics relating to population, agricultural productivity, national economy or such general information.

2. ***Common proverbs and expressions*** - Common proverbs and expressions easily enter into the public domain, and there will be no need to search painstakingly for the person who originated them.

3. ***General information*** - This refers to information available in all places where the research topic is treated and does not require any special effort to recall it.

4. ***General conclusions*** - these refer to all common and available conclusions that fall within the reach of any researcher on the subject of investigation.

The final advice that would be beneficial to all researchers is to ensure that borrowed information, whether in its original form or in the form of a paraphrase, should be acknowledged. Sometimes, the researcher may find himself acknowledging what should not have been acknowledged. This is better than not acknowledging what should be acknowledged. So the easy way out of plagiarism is: when in doubt, it is always golden to acknowledge!

Eleven

WRITING THE ABSTRACT

Meno: Yes, Socrates, but how do you mean that we do not learn but that what we call learning is recollection? Can you teach me how this is so?

- **Plato, Meno**

Ignorance is thus no longer simply opposed to knowledge: it is itself a radical condition, an integral part of the very structure of knowledge.

- **Shoshana Felman**

Writing an abstract is a necessity in the research and writing processes. Students, especially those engaged in postgraduate research, will ultimately be asked to write an abstract of their thesis or dissertation.

Meaning

An abstract is a kind of summary, and summaries are prevalent in all kinds of writing. Summaries traditionally highlight the major points of a piece of work, outlining the significant details in which the main work is encapsulated. In business writing, for instance, business reports traditionally summarize the contents in what is described as an executive summary. This allows the busy executive to glance at the summary of the work before reading the entire report.

As a summary of an entire work confined to a short, informative write-up, the abstract expresses, in a nutshell, the main argument or claim of the paper, reviewing the major points covered in the paper and comments on the content and scope of the work.

In a thesis or dissertation situation, the abstract shows the reader the main thrust of the work. The nature and strength of the abstract and the writer's ability to state the overview of the entire work in a paragraph convinces the reader that the writer has a complete grasp of the subject.

Though the abstract is usually inserted at the beginning of the research, it should be the last section of the paper to be written. It is, therefore, important to remember that a researcher should embark on the writing of the abstract only after the entire paper has been written, proof-read, revised and seen as ready for presentation.

Writing the abstract is not restricted to thesis and dissertation writing. In academic writing, an abstract, is needed in essays, articles, and reviews. Some journals demand an abstract of a paper intended for submission before deciding on whether that paper will be appropriate for publication in the journal. Before submitting a paper for presentation in a conference the organizers usually demand the abstract of the intended paper before accepting or rejecting the paper. In fact, it has become traditional to publish a book of abstracts in a conference proceeding.

Length of Abstracts

Some academic disciplines stipulate the possible length of an abstract. For instance, the APA Style Manual recommends that an abstract should not be longer than 120 words and should be confined to a paragraph. So the writer should understand that the problem of choice is necessary to enable him to determine the elements of the paper he considers most important.

When the length of the abstract is not mentioned by the authorities for whom the research is being undertaken or the academic institution where the thesis or dissertation is to be submitted, it is recommended that the whole abstract be encapsulated in a paragraph or/or confined to between one hundred and three hundred words.

For a neophyte, the best way to approach the abstract is to structure exactly the same way as the thesis or dissertation. That means that the summary should start with the introduction. Then continue with the methods, results, discussion and conclusions. By this method, the researcher picks the most important points from the sections of the paper and summarizes them appropriately to reflect the demands of the abstract.

Types of Abstracts

There are two broad types of abstracts: descriptive abstracts and informative abstracts. The main aim of descriptive abstracts is to apprise the reader of the information contained in the report or article. In the descriptive abstract, it is mandatory to include the purpose of the study, the methods used, and the scope of the work undertaken. Here, it is not necessary to provide the results, conclusions or recommendations of the study. Descriptive Abstracts serve as an introduction to the reader who will necessarily read the material to discern the results, conclusions and recommendations.

Informative abstracts are meant to communicate specific information from the report to the reader in a peculiarly succinct form. As a result, it includes the purpose, methods used, and the scope of the report, in addition to the results, conclusions and recommendations made by the researcher. Because informative abstracts provide information from every major section of the report, it is usually longer than the descriptive abstract. It is generally recommended that informative abstracts should not be more than ten percent of the length of the full report and, of course not more than three or four pages. Hence, introductory explanations, definitions and other background information should be omitted from the report.

Valuable Hints on Writing the Abstract

There are six significant pieces of information necessary in the construction of the abstract. The first is the purpose of the work. This should contain the main idea of the writer expressed in one or two sentences. The second point is the statement of the scope, focus, or concentration of the work, especially the area that requires significant attention. The third point is the method. This should detail the methodology used, and the author should make great efforts to convince the reader that the method used has concrete validity and, in fact, is the most appropriate method to be used in the study. The fourth point demands the statement of the results of the research and the conclusion reached. The fifth point is the presentation of the solutions while the last point is the statement of appropriate recommendations. Because the abstract is supposed to be a succinct piece, these six significant pieces of information could each be encapsulated in very few sentences. Furthermore, since the ideas are closely related, it will be quite appropriate to combine some sentences, but it is necessary to carefully steer them into one generic meaning.

Qualities of a Good Abstract

A good abstract should meet the following specifications:

1. The researcher must meet the word count limitation. If it is unnecessarily too long, it is a signal that the writer does not have a good grasp of the subject.

2. The abstract should be written in well-developed paragraphs that will make it coherent, concise and unified.

3. The body of the paper and the chronology of the report should be carefully followed.

4. Do not add any information that does not appear in the main paper. To ensure that the results of the research are not over-simplified, the researcher should use 'weasel-words" like "might", "may", "could", and "seems" to concretize information.

5. Passive verbs should be used mainly to emphasize the information being given as well as tone down the author.

6. It is necessary for the researcher to ensure that the most important information are clearly stated while at the same time eliminating bombastic and incoherent words.

7. Acronyms, abbreviations, symbols and technical terms that would need explanation for clarity should be avoided in the abstract.

8. The abstract should be carefully revised to ensure that it sounds like a mini-essay.

9. During the final editing and revision, the researcher should ensure that the abstract is written in the same voice as the main paper.

A GLOSSARY OF RESEARCH TERMS

A

Abstract - A summary of an article, thesis, or dissertation which usually appears at the beginning of the material.

- A type of index which gives information on the location of an article or a book, as well as a brief summary of that article.
- Databases and indexes also contain abstracts that can help the researcher decide the relevance of an article for the research being undertaken.

Acronym - A word formed by combining the initial letters or syllables of words and pronounced as a word instead of a series of letters.

Active learning – A systematic method of enquiry which gives rise to research.

Ampersand - The symbol "&" meaning "and".

Analysis - A separation of a whole into constituents in order to study its main constituents or the structure of the whole.

Annotation - An explanatory, informative, or critical note about the contents of a book or scholarly article.

Annotated bibliography - A list of sources that gives pertinent information and a short description of each source located for research. Some annotations describe the content and scope of the source, while others provide an evaluation of the quality and usefulness of the source.

Anthology - A collection of writings by different scholars compiled into a book.

APA - American Psychological Association; a system of documentation approved by this association.

Appendix - The section of a book containing supplementary materials.

Applied research - also called directed research. A kind of research that yields a systematic order of enquiry.

Article - A complete piece of nonfiction writing published in a scholarly journal.

B

Basic research - An exploration into the unknown. Also called fundamental research.

Bibliography- A list of sources used in the course of research. It is usually inserted at the end of the work, with each entry providing publication information of each source so the reader can refer to them if need be.

- A list of books recommended for reading on a given topic.

Bibliometrics - An investigative technique that uses quantitative analysis and statistical data to describe patterns of publications within a particular academic area.

Blog - Shortened form of Web log.

Blurb - A writing containing promotional information inserted on the jacket or back of a book.

Book number - Last letter or number combination in the call number of a library book, which stands for the author of the book.

Boolean operators - The words and, or, and not which are used in databases or search engines to relate the contents of two or more sets of data in different ways.

C

Call number – The identification number which indicates where a book or other library material is located in the library.

Catalogue - A database which contains information about the materials in the library and their various locations. Catalogues are usually searched by author, title, subject heading, or keyword, and they provide a basic description of the item.

Chicago Style - Chicago Manual of Style, a documentation style invented by the University of Chicago.

Citation - A reference to an article, book, or Web page which provides information to allow the reader retrieve the source.

Citation management software - Computer programmes that store bibliographic references and notes.

Citation trail - A network of citations formed when one reference work refers to sources which also refer to other sources. Also see Domino theory.

Cite - To provide a reference to a source.

Class number - The identification number which determines where a book or other library material is located in the library.

Cliché - An expression that has lost its power because of overuse. Should be avoided in research.

Colophon - A publisher's emblem; an inscription at the end of a book which gives information on the type of print, paper, and other pertinent information concerning the publication.

Copyright - The legal right which allows one control of the production, use and sale of an artistic work.

Corporate author - An organization, institution or corporation identified as the author of a book.

Cross reference - A reference from one word or term in a book or index to another word or term.

D

Database - A collection of data usually containing bibliographic citations, descriptive abstracts, full-text documents, or a combination of these, organized for retrieval.

Deductive reasoning - A form of logical reasoning which allows the forming of conclusions after relating a specific fact to a generalization.

Descriptors - Terms assigned by compilers of a database to describe the subject content of a document.

Documentary research - A research method dedicated to the learning of new facts through the study of documents and records.

DOI – Digital Object Identifier.

Discipline - An academic area like Theatre Arts, Music, Physics or Psychology.

Domino theory- The method of one research material leading to another through the process of documentation. See also *Citation trail*.

E

Edition - All copies of a book printed from a single type-setting.

Ellipsis Three spaced periods that indicate either a pause or the omission of material from a direct quotation.

Ethos - The use of language to demonstrate the trustworthiness, good intentions and penetrating knowledge of the writer.

Exigence - The circumstance that compels one to write.

F

Field – An area of study, an academic discipline; A particular area in a database where the same information is usually recorded.

ftp – Abbreviation for file transfer protocol, which means a set of guidelines establishing the format in which files can be transmitted from computer to computer.

Footnotes - Identification of reference sources used in a research report, and placed at the bottom of the page or end of a chapter.

Frontispiece - An illustration or portrait facing the title of a book.

Full text A complete document contained in a database or a Web site.

G

Genre - A literary classification identified by its own conventions.

Glossary - A list, complete with definitions of technical terms used in the text.

H

Historical research - A research technique that utilizes the historical method.

Hits - A list of results called up by a search of a database, Website, or Internet.

Holdings - The exact items owned by a library. It refers to specific issues of periodicals in a library and usually listed in a library's catalogue.

Hyperlink - A Web address that is entrenched in an electronic document and usually highlighted by colour and underlining so users can move between Web pages or sites.

Hypertext - A computer based text retrieval system which allows users to move to other parts of that document or to other Web documents.

Hypothesis - An intelligent guess, a tentative explanation which is used by the researcher as a basis for further investigation.

I

Inductive reasoning - The reasoning process that begins with facts and observations and moves to general principles from where the facts and observations are derived from.

Imprint – Information containing the place of publication, publisher, publication or copyright date of a published book.

Index - The alphabetical listing of the subjects discussed in the book, with corresponding page number usually located at the back of the book.

A separate publication pointing to information available in other sources.

Introduction - A description of the subject matter of a book which makes preliminary statements describing the main contents of the book.

Italics – A kind of typescript usually used for emphasis.

J

Journal - A scholarly periodical issued either monthly or quarterly, containing articles written for specialized or scholarly people.

K

Keyword - A word used to search a library database, Web site or the Internet, and works by matching the search word to an item in the medium being searched.

L

Library catalogue A database containing information about the materials in a library and their appropriate locations.

Logical operators - Words used to broaden or narrow an electronic database search.

Longitudinal survey – A kind of survey technique that uses trend studies, cohort studies and panel studies for survey research.

Library of Congress System - A major library classification system which helps researchers to easily locate a source from a library.

Literature review - A detailed survey of published and unpublished research in a research topic, which identifies the most significant publications in a topic, categorize and comment on them to give the reader an overview of the state of the art in the area and to show that the researcher is aware of previous research in the area of investigation.

M

Magazine A type of periodical that contains articles, and intended for a general audience. It differs from a journal which is directed to a specialized audience.

Microfiche -Flat sheets of microfilm.

Microfilm - A reproduction of texts in reduced sizes stored in a film, read on a special machine usually in the library.

Microform - A process used to reproduce texts in reduced size filmed on plastic and called microfilm.

MLA - Abbreviation for Modern Languages Association, the publishers of the method of documentation with that name.

N

Normative research - A kind of research based entirely on the impressionistic observations of the investigator.

Nall hypothesis - Latin for nullus (not any). A tentative answer to a research question, stated in the opposite form.

Number Systems - Methods of documentation used primarily in science disciplines.

O

Original research - Research that is not based on a synthesis of previous investigation.

Outline - A listing of topics meant to be covered in a research project.

P

Peer review - A process whereby experts in a particular field assess articles written by their peers to determine their suitability for publication in a particular journal. It is usually arranged in such a way that reviewers do not know the author of the document being reviewed.

Periodical - A publication like magazines, journals, newspapers, newsletters, issued at regular intervals.

Preface - A medieval Latin word, praefatia, meaning "say before." Preliminary statements in which the author states his purpose in writing the book, and acknowledging pop

1. Insert t

N

Normative research – A kind of research based entirely on the impressionist observations of the investigator.

Null hypothesis – Latin for nullus (not any). A tentative answer to a research question, stated in the opposite form.

Number System – Method of documentation used primarily in science disciplines.

O

Original research – Research that is not based on a synthesis of previous investigation.

Outline – A listing of topics meant to be covered in a research project.

P

Peer review – A process whereby experts in a particular field assess article written by their peers to determine their suitability for publication in a particular journal. It is usually arranged in such a way that reviewers do not know the author of the document being reviewed.

Periodical – A publication like magazines, journals, newspapers, newspaper, issued at regular intervals.

Preface – A medieval Latin word, *praefatia,* meaning "say before". Prelinary statement in which the author states his purpose writing the book, and acknowledge people who assisted him in the preparation of the book.

Periodical index – A list of all articles published in a magazine in a magazine or journal. This could be available in printed form or online databases.

Plagiarism – A process of copying another person's thoughts, ideas or statements without acknowledge, or submitting another person's work as one's own original work.

Primary source – An original source containing materials considered for research in a particular area or topic.

Q

Quotation – Direct use of someone's spoken or written words in the research report.

R

Record – Items in a database containing information about the books and articles which researchers can search for in a database.

Referred publication – A scholarly publication where articles submitted for publication are subjected to assessment through the process of peer review. Referred publication are usually very highly respected in research circles.

Reference – A source identified by a researcher and quoted in a research paper or article.

- A section of a library where reference materials like dictionaries, enclopedias, handbooks, directories and other references are stored.

Refutation – The art of opposing a point of view by discussing the view and showing why they are considered unsatisfactory.

Reprint – Copies of an edition of a book printed at a later time, probably after the ones printed earlier have been sold out.

Rhetorical appeal – The process of persuasion in argumentative writing whereby reason, authority, or emotion and used in advancing the argument.

Rogerian argument – A method of argumentation emphasizing the importance of withholding judgment of the other person's ideas until they are fully understood. The progenitor of this method is Carl. R. Rogers, a psychologist.

S

Scholarly journal – A journal that is primarily intended for scholars of a particular discipline. They are usually referred, and the articles contained in them are considered appropriate for research purposes.

Scope – The range of material covered in a book or article.

Search engine – A computer programmed used for searching for materials on the internet or website.

Secondary source – A source whose analysis relies on primary sources.

Serial – Publications usually issued in a series and on continuing or regular basis.

Series – Publications that are considered similar in format and content.

Short-title – The first part of compound title.

Stacks – Groups of shelves where books are placed in the library.

Subject heading – A word or phrase assigned to an item in a database which describes the content of the item.

Surveys – Non-experimental, descriptive research method of obtaining facts about a current situation through sampling a population.

Sub-title – The second part of a compound title usually explains the short title.

Syllogism – Kind of deductive reasoning that consists of two premises and a conclusion.

Synthesis – Method of collection and connection of information on a topic and usually involves summary, interpretation and analysis.

T

Table of contents – A list of chapters or part of a book in numerical order, complete with the pages on which these contents are located.

Theme – The main idea in a literary work.

Thesis – The central or main idea of a research project.

Thesaurus – Greek word – thesaurus, meaning storehouse. A list of the subject headings that are used to describe an item in particular catalogue or database.

- A book that lists words and their relationship to each other in meaning, as well as providing their synonyms and antonyms.

Theoretical framework – A short write-up containing the framework of a research work and which determines the things to be measured and the data necessary for the achievement of results in a research project.

Title page – The page in front of a book or research report which gives the title of the book, the author, and the imprint.

Tone – The attitude of the writer towards the subjects of investigation usually conveyed through the writer's choice of words and structure of sentences.

Transition – Words, phrase, sentences and paragraphs used to relate ideas by linking them to larger segments of writing.

Truncation – A shortened version of a search term.

U

URL – Abbreviation for Uniform Resource Locator. An Internet address which consists of the protocol type, the domain name and an extension of letters and numbers to identify the exact source of page within the domain.

V

Vertical file – Files containing ephemeral materials like pictures, pamphlets and newspaper clippings not listed in the card catalogue.

Volume file – A form of book containing printed sheet put together.

All these issues of periodical bound together as a unit. One book which constitute a part of series.

W

Wild card – A symbols used for the substitution of any letter or combination of letters in a search word or phrase.

REFERENCES

Addington, David W. "Data for the Theatre" in Empirical Research in Theatre No. 7(1981).

Altick, Richard D. The Art of Literacy Research 3rd Edition (Revised by John J. Fenstermarker) New York: W. W. Norton, 1981.

Barelson, Bernard. Content Analysis in Communication Research. New York: Free Press, 1952.

Derrida, Jacques. Of Grammatology. Baltimore: Johns Hopkins Up., 1974.

Dubin, Robert. Theory Building. New York: The Free Press, 1969.

Ellman, Maud. Psychoanalytic literacy criticism. London: longman, 1994.

Felman, Shoshana. "Psychoanalysis and Education: Teaching Terminable and Interminable". In robert con davis and Ronald schleifer, Eds. Contemporary literary criticism. New York: longman, 1994, 400-20.

Glenn. Cheryl and Loretta Gray. The writer's Harbrace Handbook. Third Edition. Boston: Thomson Higher Education, 2007.

Hauer, Mary G., Ruth C. Murray, Doris B. Dantin, and Myrtle S. Bolner. Books, Libraries, and Research. Second Edition. Dubuque, Iowa: Kendal, 1983.

Leggert, Glenn, C. David mead, and William Charvat. Prentice-Hall Handbook for Writers (Fourth Edition), Ealewood Cliffs, Prentice Hall, 1965.

Mc Neill, Patrick. Research Methods, Second Edition. London: Routledge, 1990.

Meyer, Michael. The little brown guide to writing research papers. Boston: Little, Brown and Company.

Nwabueze, Emeka, guardian of the Cosmos, Ikeja: Longman, 1990.

--------- "Ritual Drama of Appeasement: A comparative study of Soyinka and Noh" In Synthesis: Journal of Comparative poetics XVII (1990), 83-90.

------- "The Memoir as Literature: Evolutionary Meliorism in Nelson Mandela's Long Walk to Freedom". The Negro Educational Review XLIX (1998), 129-38.

--------- "Theoretical Construction and Constructive theorizing on the Execution of Ikemefuna in Achebe's Thing Fall Apart: A Study of Critical Dualism". Research in African Literature 31:2 (2000), 163-73.

-------- Ranking of African Literacy Writers and the Canonisation of Texts." Delivered at First Mary Kingsley Lecture, Main Theatre Oriental and African studies, University of London, May 20, 2000.

------- "Traditional Theatre in a Southern Africa Kingdom: Performance Aesthetic of the Umhlanga dance of Swaziland,". in Visions and Re-visions, ABIC, 2003, 94-107.

-------- Vision and Re-visions: Selected discourse on Literary Criticism, Enugu: ABIC 2013.

MLA Handbook for Writers of Research Papers. These and Dissertations. New York: Modern Languages Association, 1977.

Osborne, Alex F. applied Imagination. New York: Charles Scribner's Sons, 1957.

Plato, Meno. Trans, GM.A Grube. Indianapolis: Hackett, 1980.

Rein, Stephen. The prentice-Hall Guide for College Writers. Eight Edition. Upper Saddle Riber, NH: Pearson, 2008.

Ruggeiro, Vincent Ryan. Beyond Feeling: A guide to Critical Thinking. 7th Edition. New York: McGraw Hill, 2004.

Sanders, Chancey. An introduction to Research in English literacy History. New York: Macmillian, 1963.

Shafer, Robert Jones (Ed.) A guide to historical method. Ontario: The Dorsey Press, 1980.

Shklovsky, Victor. "Art as Technique" in I.T. Lemon and M.J. Reis (Trans. And Eds). Russian Formalist Criticism: Four Essays, University of Nebraska Press, 1965.

Ukala, Sam Manual of Research and of thesis writing in Theatre Arts. (second edition) Ibadan: Kraft Books, 2006.

vanalstyne, Judith S. Professional and Technical Writing Strategies: Communication in Technology and Science. Sixth Edition. Upper Saddle River, N.J. Pearson Education Inc., 2005.

Willis, Hulon, Writing Term paper, the Research paper, the Critical Paper. Second Edition, revised by Alan Heinemann. New York: Harcourt Brace, 1983.

Yellin, Linda L. A Sociology Writer's Guide. Boston: Pearson Education, Inc. 2009.

INDEX

A

Abstract, 151

- length, 152
- meaning of, 151
- qualities of, 154,
- types of, 153
- writing of, 154

absurdism. 14

active learning, 3

ad hominine, 92

Altarista, 27

Altick, Richard, 8

American Psychological Association style, 122

- court cases, 129
- film, 128
- in-text citation, 122
- internet sources, 130
- journal articles, 128
- personal communication, 126
- single author works, 123
- status, 129
- works by two authors, 124

analytical discourse, 40

appeals to tradition, 92

arguments

- presentation of, 90
- shaping of, 91
- things to avoid, 92

argument 1

arrangement

- categorical, 48
- chronological, 47
- methodological, 47
- thematic, 47

B

bandwagon effect, 92

bibliographic coupling, 91

bibliography, 21

bibliometrics research, 80

- areas of, 80
- definition of, 80
- laws of, 81

biographical criticism, 55

books

- review of, 48

- usefulness of, 21

C

CD-ROM, 50

Chicago Manual of Style, 137

- endnotes, 138, 139
- footnotes, 138, 139
- in-text citation, 138
- superscript in, 138

citation, 106

- bible, 109
- constitution, 109
- corporate author, 108, 114
- drama, 109
- e-mail,, 121
- poetry, 109
- three or more authorss, 108, 113
- two or three authors 107
- unknown author, 102
- works by same author, 113

conceptual analysis, 75

conclusion, 33

conference papers, 49

consistency, 98

content analysis, 77

- advantage of, 79
- definition of, 77
- disadvantages of, 79
- uses of, 78

content notes, 103

critical interpretation, 37

D

deconstruction, 56

definition, 42

dewey Decimal System, 20

dialectical research, 83

documentary research 52

- reasons for, 53
- sources of materials, 54

documentation, 101

- dissertation, 119
- journal articles, 115
- law cases, 118
- lecture, 119
- monthly magazine articles, 116
- newspaper, articles, 117
- oral interview, 120

- weekly magazine articles, 117
- thesis, 119

domino theory, 20

draft, 87

E

equivocation, 93

excite, 27

experimental research, 59

- categories of, 60

f

fact-finding, 37

false analogy, 93

false authority, 93

field experiment, 61

G

Google, 27

government reports, 49

guilt by association, 93

H

hasty generalization, 93

historical research, 57

- characteristics of, 58

- data collection in, 59

Hot Bot, 27

Hurston, Zora, 1

hypothesis, 40

I

information

- finding of, 20
- gathering of, 17

Infoseek, 27

Internet, 49

- advantages/disadvantages, 26

interview

- conducting, 66
- recording, 67
- method, 66

in-text citation, 104

- placement of, 141

introduction, 33

J

journal articles, 48

L

language, 97

library

- classification system, 20
- development, 18
- use of, 19

library of Congress System, 20

literature

- review of, 42, 45
- writing of a review, 51

Lycos, 27

M

Magazines, 50

Missing information, 142

Model, 32

Modern Languages Association, 102

N

natural experiments, 61

newspaper, 50

non sequitur, 92

normative research, 6

number systems, 130

- in chemistry, 133
- in computer science, 132
- in physics and engineering, 134

- in-text citation, 135

O

observation

- participant, 74
- response to, 72
- types of, 72
- unobtrusive, 72

observational research, 69

- ethical considerations in, 71
- necessity for, 70

observational studies, 61

outline, 29

- choice of, 32
- composing of, 31
- decimal notation of, 32
- elements of, 30
- meaning, 29
- types of, 30

over implication, 93

P

parenthetical citations, 103

participant observation,

- difficulties in, 75

- history of, 74
- meaning of, 74

passive learning, 3

plagiarism, 143

- avoidance of, 149
- intentional, 145
- meaning of, 145
- penalty for, 148
- reasons for, 147
- unintentional, 145

preliminary statements, 40

proposal, 36

publisher's imprint, 110

Q

questionnaire, 67

- designing of, 68
- validation of, 69

quotations, 110

r

red herring, 93

reference list, 126

reference works, 117

relational analysis, 78

research,
- bibliometrics, 80
- categories of, 126
- dialectical, 83
- documentary, 52
- experimental, 59
- exploratory, 82
- historical, 57
- meaning of, 4
- observational procedure, 69
- purpose of, 7
- sources, 23
- time schedule in, 44

research materials,
- availability of, 11

research report, 84

researchers
- qualities of, 8

revision technique, 95

rhetorical method, 88

S

sample
- design of, 65

sampling
- cluster, 65
- double, 65
- procedure, 63
- random, 64
- stratified, 64

scholarly activities, 37

scientific writing, 94

search engines, 27

sources
- evaluation of, 54
- internet, 25
- selection of, 24

survey research method, 62

surveys

longitudinal, 63

T

thesis
- development of, 15

theoretical framework, 42

tone, 97

topic
- controversial, 12

- manageability of, 12
- selection of, 10

W

writing

development of, 1

www.ingramcontent.com/pod-product-compliance
Lightning Source LLC
Chambersburg PA
CBHW041657040426
R18086600001B/R180866PG42333CBX00001B/1